SCULTURA II

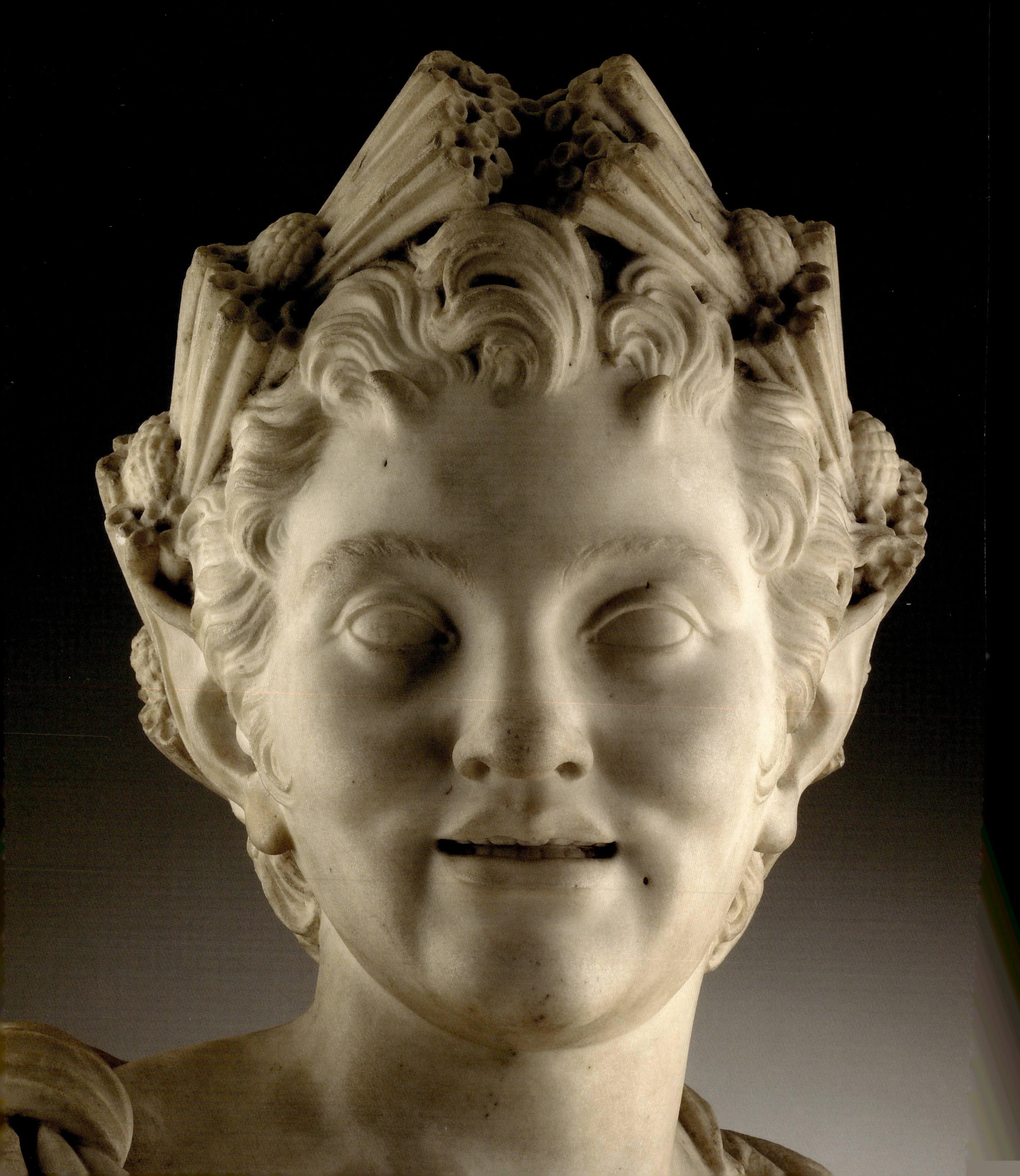

SCULTURA II
TOMASSO BROTHERS FINE ART

PAUL HOLBERTON PUBLISHING

SCULTURA II

15–24 October 2009

at Williams Moretti & Irving Gallery

24 East 80th Street

New York 10075

Tomasso Brothers Fine Art

Bardon Hall Lane, Weetwood Lane

Leeds LS16 8HJ, England

Tel. + 44 (0)113275545

info@tomassobrothers.co.uk

www.tomassobrothers.co.uk

This catalogue represents our second exhibition dedicated purely to sculpture, which is to be presented in the prestigious galleries of Williams Moretti & Irving, New York, and we would like to thank Adam, Fabrizio and Ian for extending the kind invitation to return.

We would also like to express our thanks to Sir Timothy Clifford for kindly writing the foreword to our second catalogue. We are honoured that such an illustrious gentleman as Sir Timothy has found the time to contemplate Tomasso Brothers and prepare such an insightful overview.

All three of us would once again like to extend our appreciation to Charlotte for her research, endeavours and willingness to work under intense and pressurized time-scales. Although the face of Tomasso Brothers is Dino, Johnny and Raff, discerning people will understand that we could not function without the support we receive from several different directions. To this end may we express our gratitude to Kelli, Andrew and, more recently, Tobias Desmet.

We would like to thank the following specialists and academics for their contribution to the catalogue:

Dr Charles Avery (C.A.)
Dr. Dorothea Diemer (D.D.)
Gregory Muenzen (G.M.)
Jeanette Sisk (J.S.)

Also thank you very much to Karen for all her help and understanding over the last few years.

FOREWORD

Wilting from the searing heat in Florence during late July, I dropped into the Bargello and there behind the book counter, but much in evidence, I noted a copy of SCULTURA (2008), produced by Tomasso Brothers. I would not say it constituted an oasis but it was like a welcome nod to old friends and, moreover, old friends from home. To see such a trade catalogue in the Bargello, the *sanctum santorum* of Florentine sculpture, was unexpected but it was indeed a worthy neighbour of the catalogues of the permanent collection of that august body.

Few are not now aware of the phenomenon that is Tomasso Brothers of Leeds. When I was directing the National Galleries of Scotland, I met the Tomasso brothers from time to time in the most astonishingly unlikely places in Europe and America, and they persistently asked me to visit their establishment, Bardon Hall, in Leeds. What a delight my first visit was – a large Victorian villa with the ground floor brimful of sculpture, plinths, parade furniture, and a miscellaneous collection of paintings, drawings and books. How lucky we are that so many Italians have chosen to come and live in Britain! They are so often hardworking, intelligent, and intensely creative, but retaining much of their native genius, which overlays their British education. The Tomassos are real Leeds people, with Leeds accents and supporting the Leeds Football Club, but they are also essentially Italian in their vitality, ambition, acuity, love of food and drink – and indeed their overriding passions. My grandson, aged nearly five, announced to me recently that he would like to be an Italian; my wife and I rather agree with him.

This is an exhibition of fine sculptures, well presented and well catalogued, but it is not a metropolitan effort. It is astonishing that this contribution is not from dealers in London, Paris or New York, and that makes it all the more admirable. Would that my fellow countrymen, or indeed British museums and galleries, collected more Italian sculpture, for it constitutes overwhelmingly the *crème de la crème* of European sculpture. So I hope that those who may visit this show, or read this catalogue, will share with me in some of the pleasures that these works of art exude.

SIR TIMOTHY CLIFFORD

SCULTURA II

1. ITALIAN, 14th century, *Pair of Stylobate Lions*
2. ANTONIO RIZZO (attributed to), *Pietà with Mourning Angels*
3. ITALIAN, last quarter of the 15th century, *Pair of Angels holding Candlesticks*
4. MODERNO (GALEAZZO MONDELLA), *The Virgin and Child with Saints Anthony Abbot and Jerome*
5. FLORENTINE, *c.* 1500, *A Seated Lion*, probably after the Marzocco of Florence
6. FLORENTINE, first quarter of the 16th century, *Bust of an Unknown Young Man*
7. FLORENTINE, third quarter of the 16th century
   (GIOVAN) BATTISTA LORENZI (attributed to)
   Alexander the Great as Jupiter Ammon
8. ROMAN, late 16th century, cast from [lost] models of *c.* 1550
   attributed to MICHELANGELO BUONAROTTI
   The Good and the Bad Thieves, from the Crucifixion
9. GIAMBOLOGNA, *Prometheus bringing Fire to Mankind*
10. HUBERT GERHARD, *Mounted River-god (Fountain Figure)*
11. BARTHÉLEMY PRIEUR, *Hercules slaying the Nemean Lion*
12. HUBERT LE SUEUR, *A General on Horseback*
13. GUILLAUME BERTHELOT (attributed to), *The Borghese Gladiator*
14. GIANFRANCESCO SUSINI (attributed to), *Pacing Bull*
15. ROMAN, 17th century, *The Pietà* (after Michelangelo)
16. FRANÇOIS DUQUESNOY (attributed to), *Cupid carving his Bow*

1. **ITALIAN**, 14th century

Pair of Stybolate Lions

White marble

22 in. (56 cm) high, 32 5/8 in. (83 cm) long, 12 1/4 in. (31 cm) wide

Stylized recumbent lions such as this majestic pair, which formerly constituted the bases of columns, are known as stylobate lions; a famous pair form part of the collection at the Isabella Stewart Gardner Museum, Boston. Originating in the Romanesque period, this type of column support was used throughout Europe, but especially in Italy. Stylistically the exhibition lions lie somewhere between pure Romanesque (such as the pair in Verona marble supporting the portico of Parma Cathedral) and the Renaissance set which support the monument of Vitaliano and Giovanni Borromeo in the chapel of Palazzo Borromeo, Isola Bella, Lago Maggiore. They are made of white Carrara marble and date from the late fourteenth century. Their manes have quite clearly been differentiated, one being of a fuller shape with more exuberant curls, and we may assume that they represent a lion and lioness. It is interesting to note that many of America's foremost collectors from the early to mid twentieth century strove to include examples of this type and quality of Italian sculpture in their collections.

RELATED LITERATURE

M. Natale, *I monumenti Borromeo*, Turin 1997, nos. 2, 3, 5, 137–38

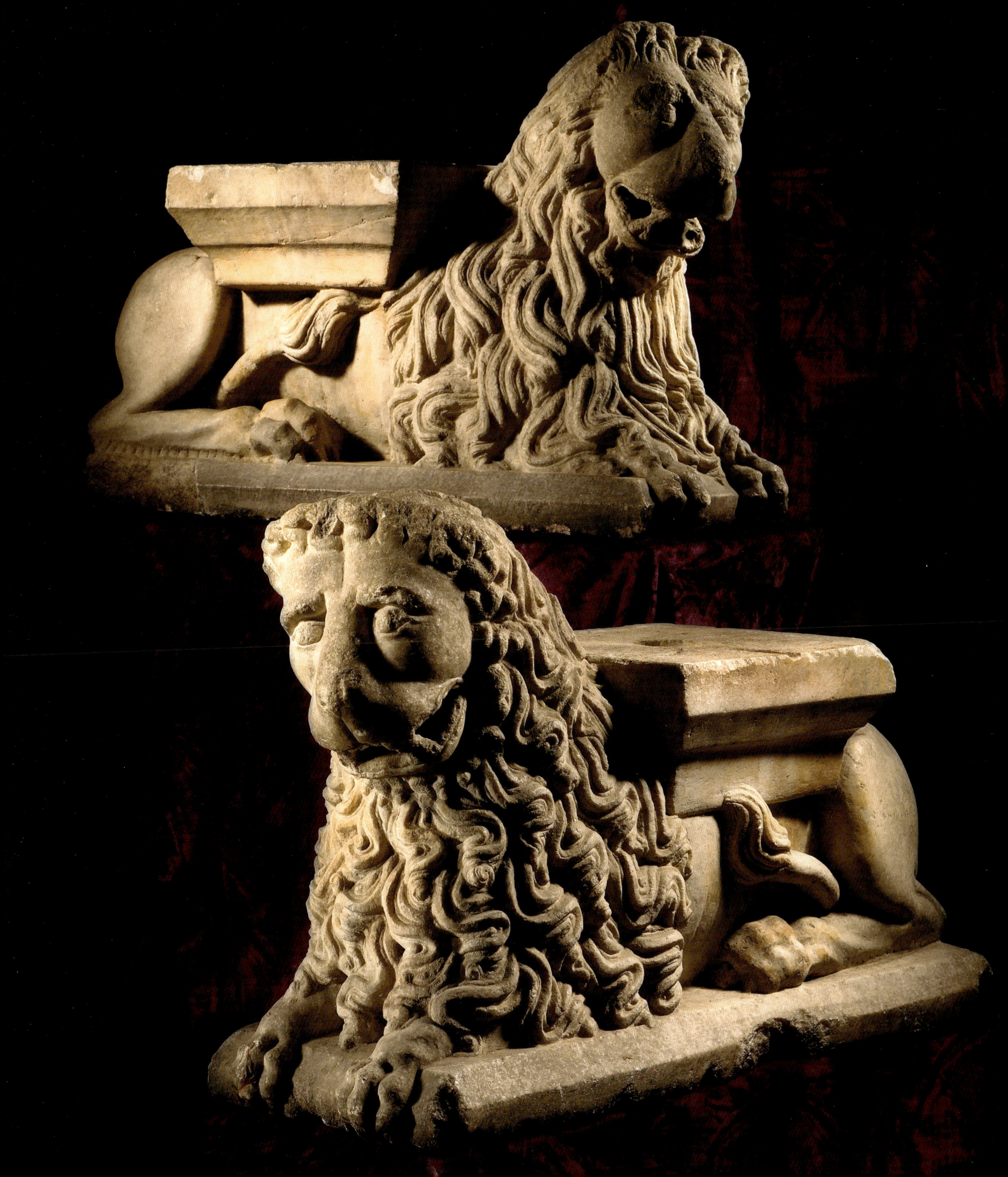

2. ANTONIO RIZZO (1425/40–1499)

(attributed to)

Pietà with Mourning Angels, 1480s

Pietra serena

24 ½ in. (62.5 cm)

In this relief, a so-called *Imago Pietatis*, the lifeless body of Christ is presented to the viewer as if on a stage, and the grief-stricken angels crying over his body are a cue for the devoted to feel the same sense of deep loss. The bottom edge of the relief, with its subtle floral carving, is an allusion to the sarcophagus in which Christ was supposed to have been lain: the moment before he was lowered into the darkness of his tomb was frequently depicted. An *Imago Pietatis* was often associated with the tabernacle of the host above the altar – Christ's supreme sacrifice being implicit in his transubstantiation into the eucharist in the mass.

The composition and material of the relief indicate that it was made in the Veneto or Padua, where the subject flourished, and in the latter city Donatello's *Man of Sorrows* relief provides one of the earliest and most influential examples, dating to the 1440s. In Venice Pietro Lombardo's Tomb of Doge Malipiero in Santi Giovanni e Paolo has a *Man of Sorrows* relief, *c.* 1480, with a similar arrangement of Christ's arms and floral border: thus the present relief would seem to come from the celebrated Lombardo workshop, which dominated late Quattrocento and early Cinquecento marble sculpture in Venice. The present relief is more idiosyncratic and pathos-ridden, however, than the sober classical vocabulary of the Lombardo. There is a subtly different vision here. An artist who had worked on the Doge Malipiero tomb, the celebrated sculptor Antonio Rizzo, may be responsible for its creation, since the relief shows some of his stylistic signatures.

The broad, squared torso compares favourably to that of his masterpiece, the *Adam* of the Arco Foscari in the Doge's Palace, Venice, with its high knotted ribcage, taut anatomy and pinched waist. Also shared are the wide-set cheekbones with open mouth and exposed teeth. The stylization of the heavy lids of Christ's eyes is similarly found in the accompanying *Eve* statue, the pair dating from *c.* 1485. The stylized veins of the arms are comparable to those of Rizzo's *Risen Christ* marble in the Tomb of Doge Niccolò Tron in the Frari. Rizzo looked to medieval sculpture as well as the Florentine masters like Donatello and Pollaiuolo; he was a highly individual artist, whose facial types were marked by an expressionistic depth, with deeply incised brows evoking a particular melancholic introspection, also evident here.

There is a tender evocation of grief by the two angels of the relief as they support the nearly lifeless body of Christ, their mouths frozen agape in horror. There is a tenderly observed finesse to the carving of Christ's hair, and a vein highlighted on his forehead. The notched hatching of the eyebrow and pointed fingers are all characteristics of Rizzo. The angels' soft, *mouillé* drapery is also typical and provides an apt complement to Christ's écorché-like arms, hardened after the ordeal of his crucifixion, to which the nail-holes in his palms refer. The artist balances this poignant expressionism with a harmonious rhythm of

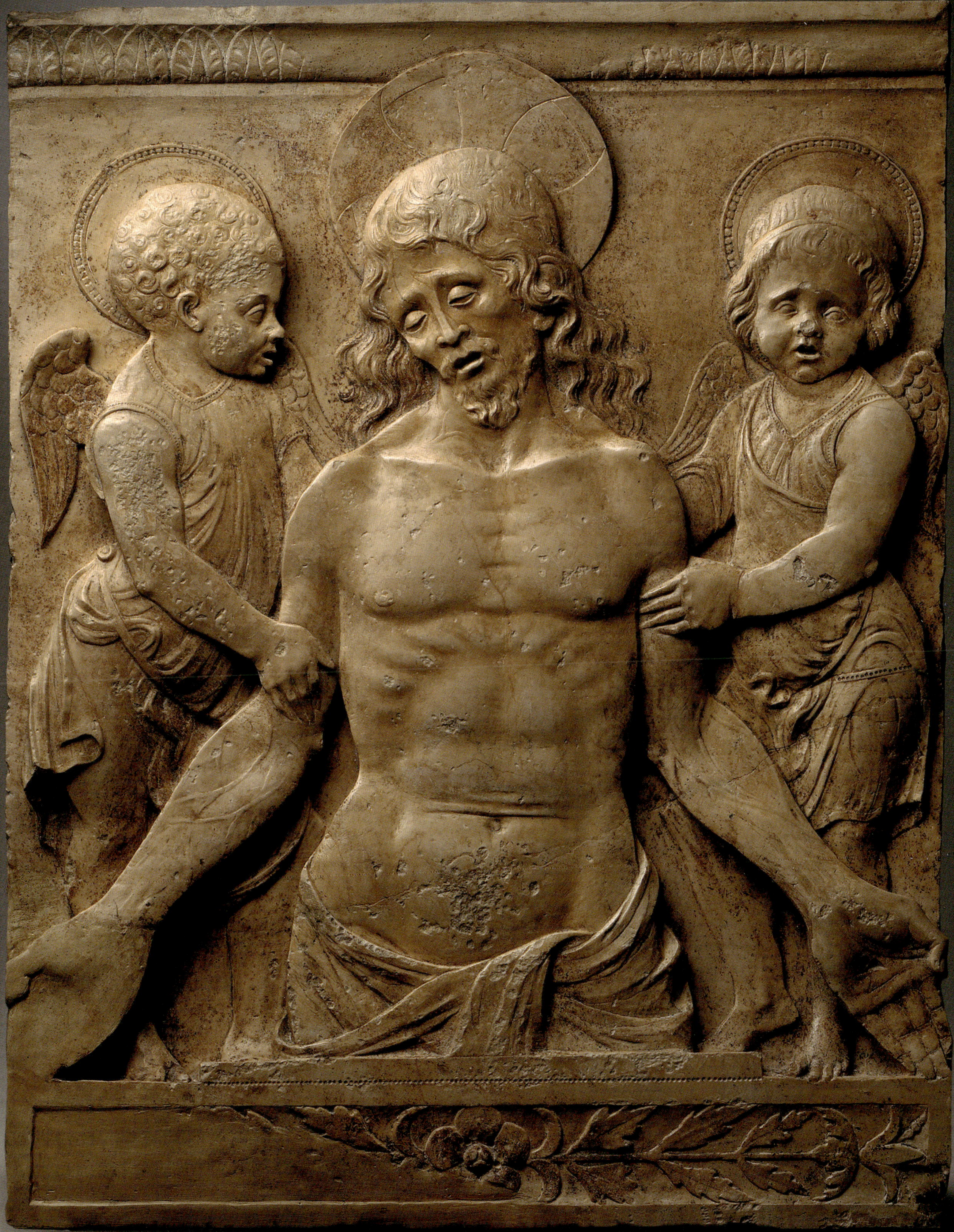

forms: the distinctly rounded shapes of the three heads are repeated in their halos and further echoed by the arcs and circular forms of Christ's abdomen; these alternate with the strong diagonals created by the arms of all the figures, creating a complex yet balanced arrangement. At the very centre of this static X-shaped composition, striking by its very discordance, this accomplished artist has placed the gently falling head of Christ, eyelids fluttering before they close. G.M.

RELATED LITERATURE

A. Markham Schulz, *Antonio Rizzo: Sculptor and Architect*, Princeton, New Jersey, 1983, figs. 39, 48, 105

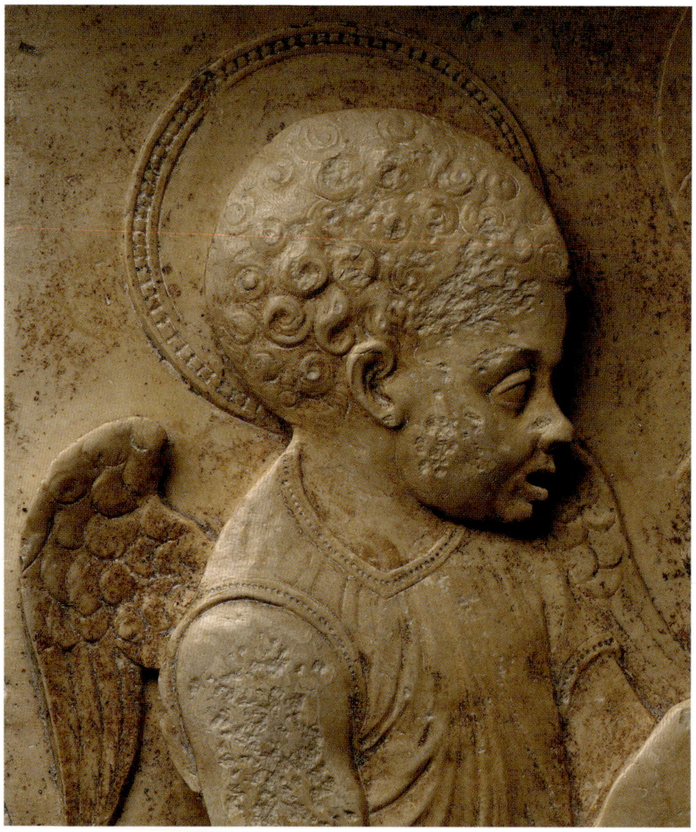

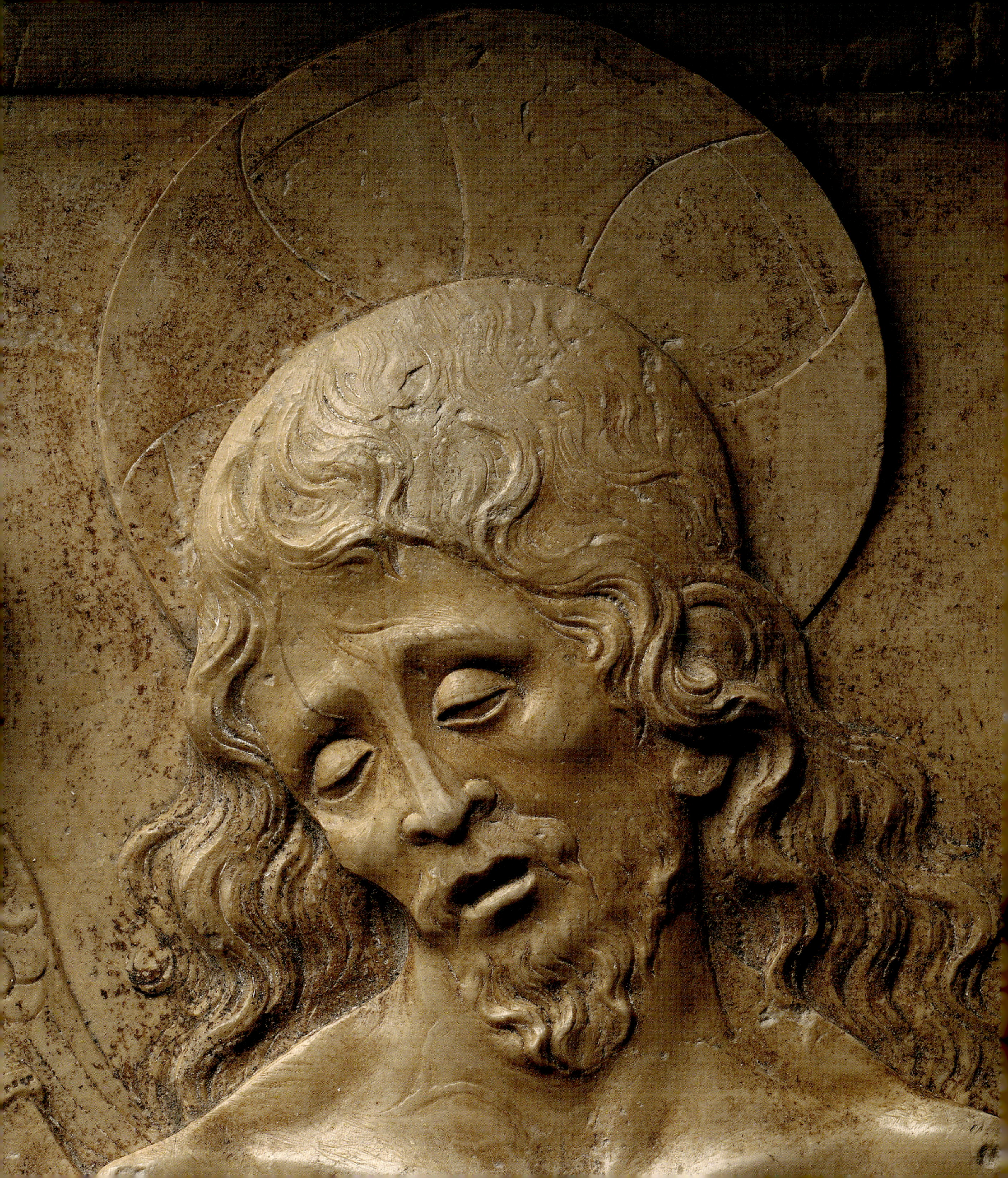

3. ITALIAN, last quarter of the 15th century

Pair of Angels holding Candlesticks

Marble

17.5 in. (44.5 cm) high

In form and scale this charming pair of angels recalls one of Michelangelo's earliest sculptural works, the *Angel holding a Candlestick* from the Arca of Saint Dominic in the Church of San Domenico Maggiore in Bologna, made in 1494–95 as a pendant to an already existing angel carved by the recently deceased master-sculptor Niccolò dell'Arca. Like the Bologna pair, the present angels are shown kneeling and looking out over one shoulder as they support on raised knee a large candlestick designed to accommodate a real wax candle. Our pair was probably intended to be placed upon an altar but could have adorned another type of sculptural monument in a church setting.

The angels' long, flowing garments, belted at the waist and gathered around the hips, with loops of fabric encircling their shoulders, are comparable to other representations of angels dating from the late fifteenth century in Italy, and more specifically to the costume worn by Michelangelo's Bologna figure. J.S.

RELATED LITERATURE

J. Pope-Hennessy, *Italian High Renaissance and Baroque Sculpture*, London and New York 1985, pp. 301–02, pl. 1

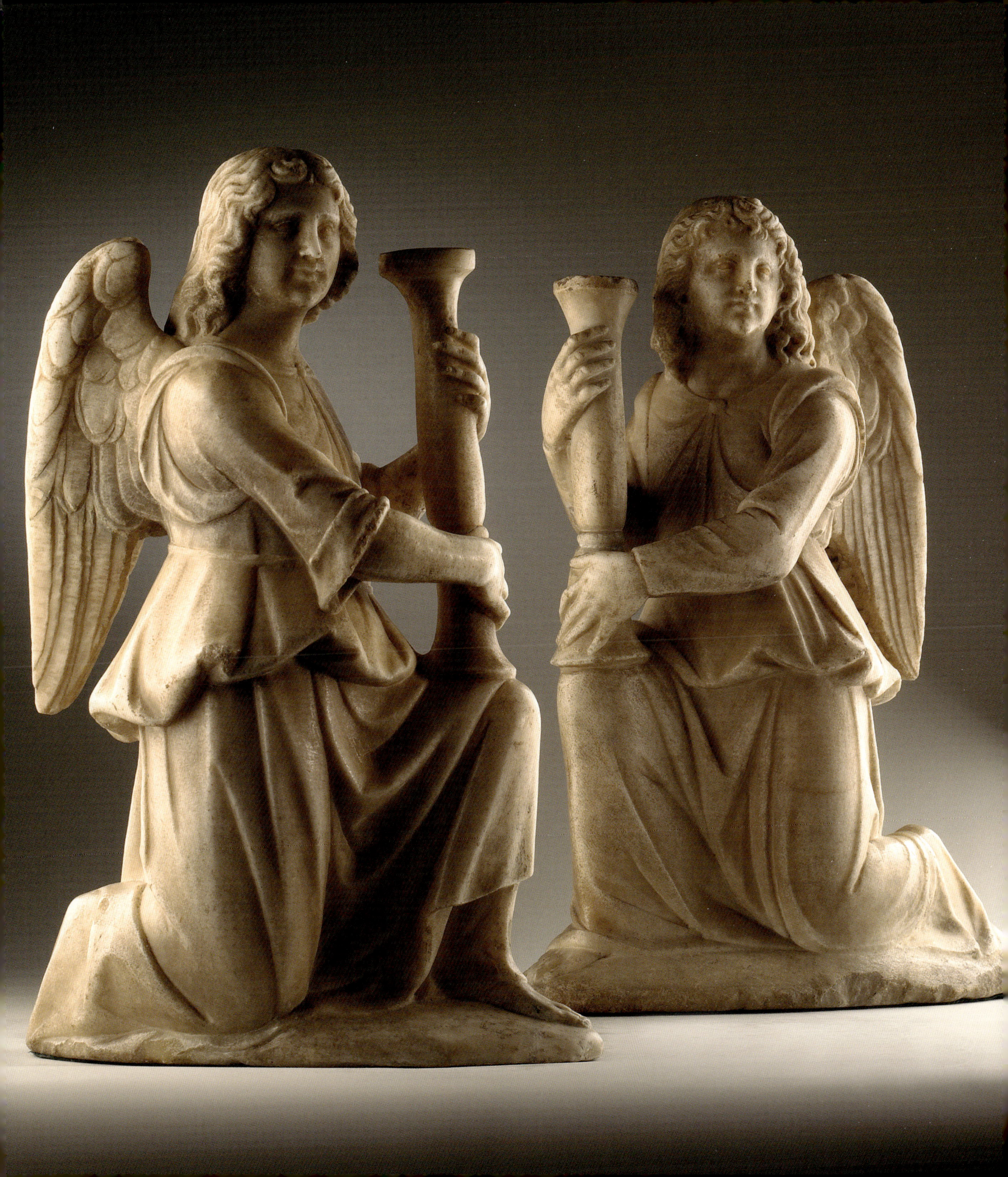

4. MODERNO (GALEAZZO MONDELLA) (1467–1528)

The Virgin and Child with Saints Anthony Abbot and Jerome, c. 1490

Cast and chased silver, partially gilt

4 ⅕ in. (10.6 cm) high, 2 ½ in. (6.4 cm) wide

PROVENANCE: Sigmund Morganroth collection, Chicago

Moderno was undoubtedly the master of the Renaissance plaquette. Approximately forty-five extant works are attributed to this master; some of them are signed *Modernus fecit*, others with variations of this. His work is quite clearly influenced by the eminent painter Andrea Mantegna, with whose work he must have come into contact when travelling to Ferrara and Mantua. The impact of Venetian art – the work of Cima, for example – is also evident, as is that of the great Brescian painter Vincenzo Foppa. The combination of these stylistic inspirations, along with classical influences deriving from Raphael and his circle, led to a highly sophisticated style.

Galeazzo Mondella's sobriquet 'Moderno' was probably chosen by him in order to distinguish himself against his contemporary and rival the great Mantuan sculptor Pier Jacopo Alari Bonacolsi, called 'Antico'.

A high percentage of Moderno's plaquettes are made in bronze, although two masterpieces by him in the Kunsthistorisches Museum, Vienna, *The Flagellation of Christ* and a *Madonna and Child with Saints*, are, like the exhibition piece, parcel-gilt silver. The medium of silver lends itself to the meticulous quality needed successfully to convey a complex, full and highly refined image on a small scale. Of all the versions of this composition, the exhibition plaquette, being in silver, allows us to appreciate fully the skill and craftsmanship of the artist. The highly decorated *aedicula*, around which the two saints are arranged in adoration of the Virgin and Child, is beautifully designed, making this an example of a small-scale work of art that transcends the boundaries of sculpture, draughtsmanship and metalwork.

RELATED LITERATURE

U. Middledorf and O. Goetz, *Medals and Plaquettes from the Sigmund Morgenroth Collection*, Chicago 1944, p. 151, nos. 222, 223

G. Toderi and F. Vannel, *Placchette: Secoli XV–XVIII nel Museo Nazionale del Bargello*, Florence 1996, p. 88, nos. 155–56; p. 89, no. 157

F. Trevisani and D. Gasparotto, *Bonacolsi l'Antico. Uno Scultore nella Mantova di Mantegna e Isabella d'Este*, exh. cat., Palazzo Ducale, Mantua, 13 September 2008–6 January 2009, p. 91, fig 4

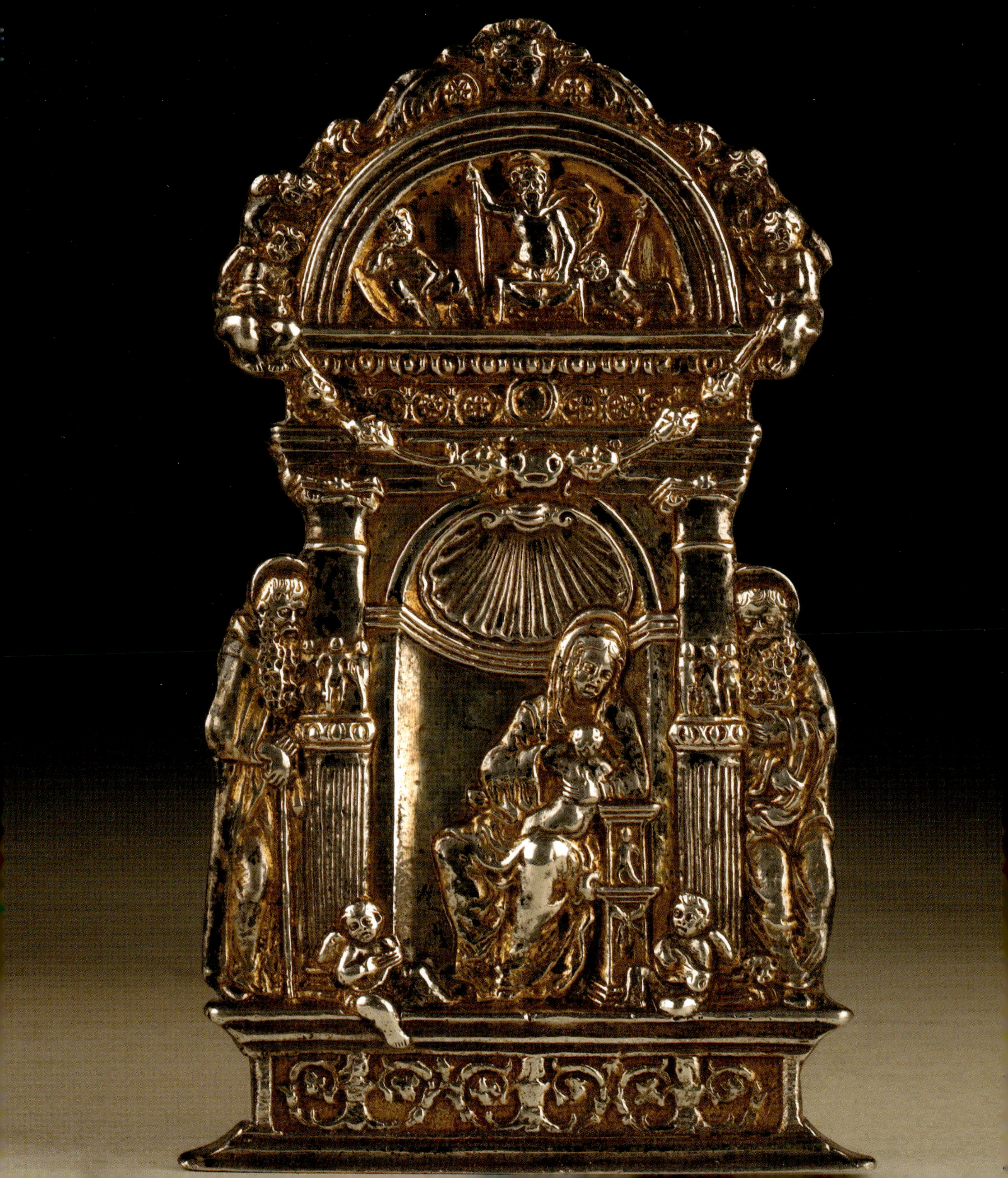

5. FLORENTINE, *c.* 1500

A Seated Lion, probably after the Marzocco of Florence

Bronze

3 ⅜ in. (8.6 cm) high

This small but impressive statuette appears to be unpublished. In pose and demeanour (apart from the turn of its head in the opposite direction) it resembles the civic lion of Florence – a stone, sometimes gilded, or marble statue that has long stood like a symbolic sentry at the corner of the dais (*ringhiera*) in the Piazza della Signoria. This is sometimes known as the 'Marzocco', because it resembles the winged lion that is the symbol of St Mark.

Presumably because the last of a long line of statues of the civic lion had, like its predecessors, weathered away, the Marzocco was replaced after 1812 with a similar lion carved in grey sandstone (*pietra serena*) by the great Donatello. This had been made in 1418 to ornament the newel-post of the stairs to the papal apartment in the monastery of Santa Maria Novella, which were demolished a century later. It supports with a forepaw a shield bearing the civic arms, a fleur-de-lys or iris (*il giglio*). In 1885 Donatello's original was removed to the Museo del Bargello for the sake of conservation and replaced with the present cast in bronze.

The Marzocco's appearance seems to vary over the years in paintings, not just with the styles of successive periods or artists, but also probably because the stone beast had periodically to be replaced and its own style changed in the process. The earliest depiction is in an anonymous painting of the martyrdom of Savonarola in 1497 (Museo di San Marco, Florence), closely followed by a fresco showing *The Confirmation of the Rule* by Domenico Ghirlandaio in Santa Trinita (Brucker 1983, p. 135, pl. XX). There are other appearances, in the background of Piero di Cosimo's portrait of an anonymous soldier – presumably a member of the national guard – in the National Gallery, London (inv. no. 895; datable after 1504, given that Michelangelo's *David* is also shown *in situ*); in Giovanni Stradano's fresco of *The Return of the Medici in 1513* on the walls of the Palazzo della Signoria (Del Meglio *et al.* 2005, pl. 35); a later fresco showing a firework display, at a date when Bandinelli's *Hercules and Cacus* and Cellini's *Perseus* had joined the collection of monumental statuary in the Piazza; and Vasari's *Festa degli Omaggi* (Feast of the Homages) fresco in the Sala di Gualdrada of the Apartments of Eleonora in the Palazzo Vecchio (*c.* 1555–65; Allegri and Cecchi 1980, p. 211, figs. 13, 48).

Its origins as a civic symbol are unknown. One theory holds that it was chosen as the symbol of the Guelph party, to contrast with the eagle of their deadly rivals, the Ghibellines. In any case by 1363 its status was firmly established and captives from Pisa were made to kiss its posterior.

The present statuette, seated four-square on a slightly projecting plinth, undercut at the front, distinctly resembles stone lions from newel-posts attributed to the workshop of Michelozzo di Bartolommeo, Donatello's associate, in the monasteries of Santissima Annunziata and Sant'Apollonia (Del Meglio *et al.* 2005, pls. 44–45). Yet the much more fluid hair of the mane and fuller modelling of the muzzle suggest a date towards the end of the fifteenth century and the influence of Verrocchio or Bertoldo. C.A.

COMPARATIVE LITERATURE

E. Allegri and A. Cecchi, *Palazzo Vecchio e i Medici – Guida storica*, Florence 1980

G.A. Brucker, *Firenze 1138–1737: L'impero del fiorino*, Florence 1983

A. Del Meglio, M. Carchio and R. Manescalchi, *Il Marzocco – The Lion of Florence*, Florence 2005

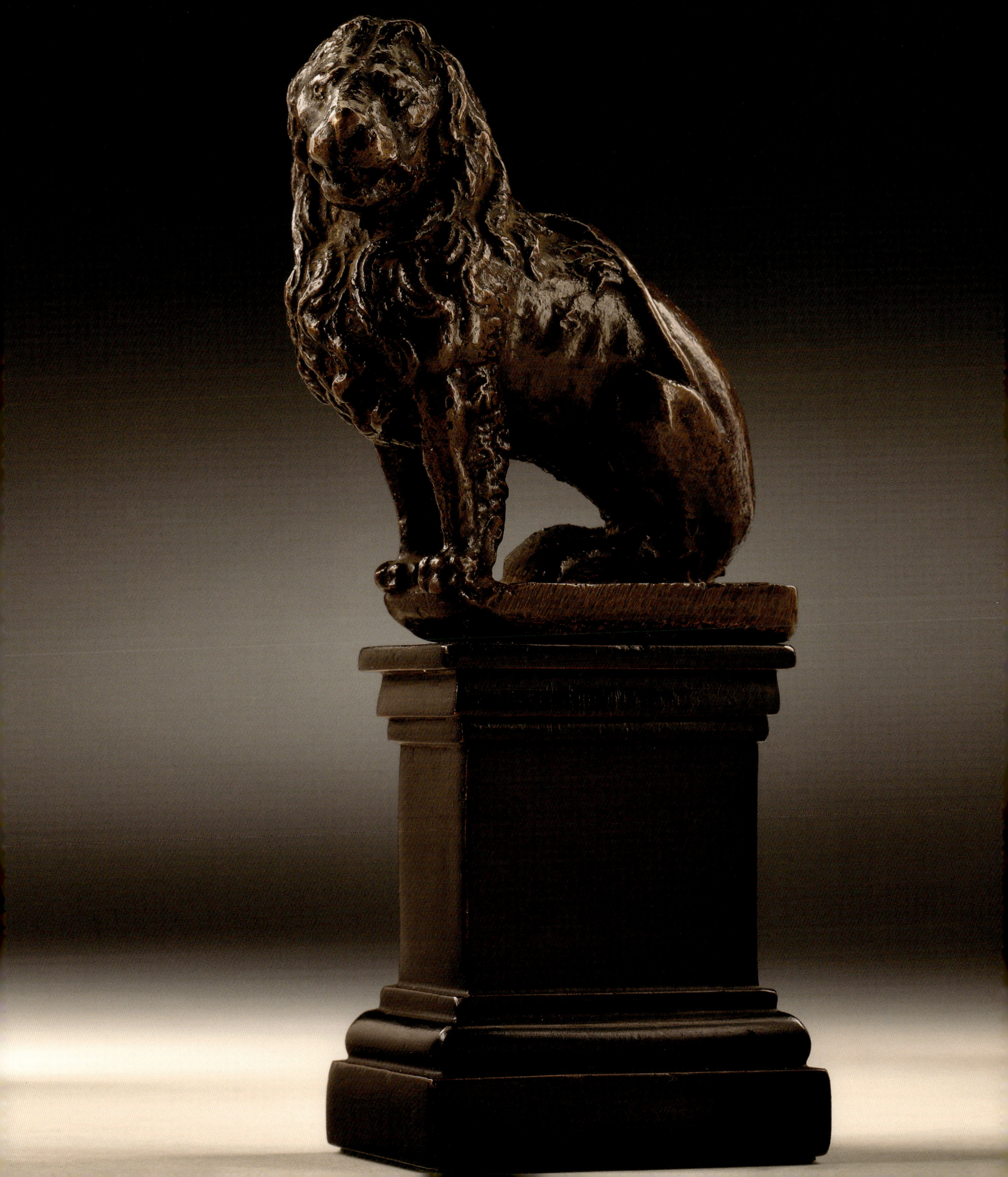

6. FLORENTINE, first quarter of the 16th century

Bust of an Unknown Young Man

Terracotta with traces of polychromy

22 3/4 in. (58 cm) high, 21 5/8 (55 cm) wide

The revival of the sculptured portrait bust was one of the great artistic developments of Italian Renaissance, and this sober portrayal of an unknown young man well represents the type of private portraiture produced in the early years of the sixteenth century. The sitter's costume is comparable to clothing worn in other portraits of the period, such as Andrea del Sarto's *Portrait of a Man (Andrea di Matteo degli Albizi?)*, painted c. 1512 and now in the collection of the Duke of Northumberland at Alnwick Castle. In both the painting and the sculpture, the slightly ruffled edges of the sitter's *camicia* are barely visible beneath the square neckline of his heavy outer garment. The large, puffed sleeves, shown only to the elbow in the bust, fit snugly along the forearms in the Del Sarto portrait. Each figure also sports a *berretta*, a type of cap that was common during the period and could be worn with the flaps up or down. In both the painting and the bust the cap is worn just above the hairline with the flaps turned up.

Although the costumes of the two sitters are quite similar, their portrayals differ significantly, owing to the character of their media. While a painted portrait can show the subject in any number of settings, by its nature a portrait bust isolates the sitter from any specific context. Like other portrait busts of the period, this is truncated just above the waist and shows only the slightest hint of movement in the head. It continues a tradition of portraiture established by Florence's greatest Renaissance sculptors of the mid fifteenth century and exemplified in the early sixteenth by artists such as Pietro Torrigiano. J.S.

RELATED LITERATURE

A. Natali, *Andrea del Sarto*, New York 1999, p. 105, pl. 91

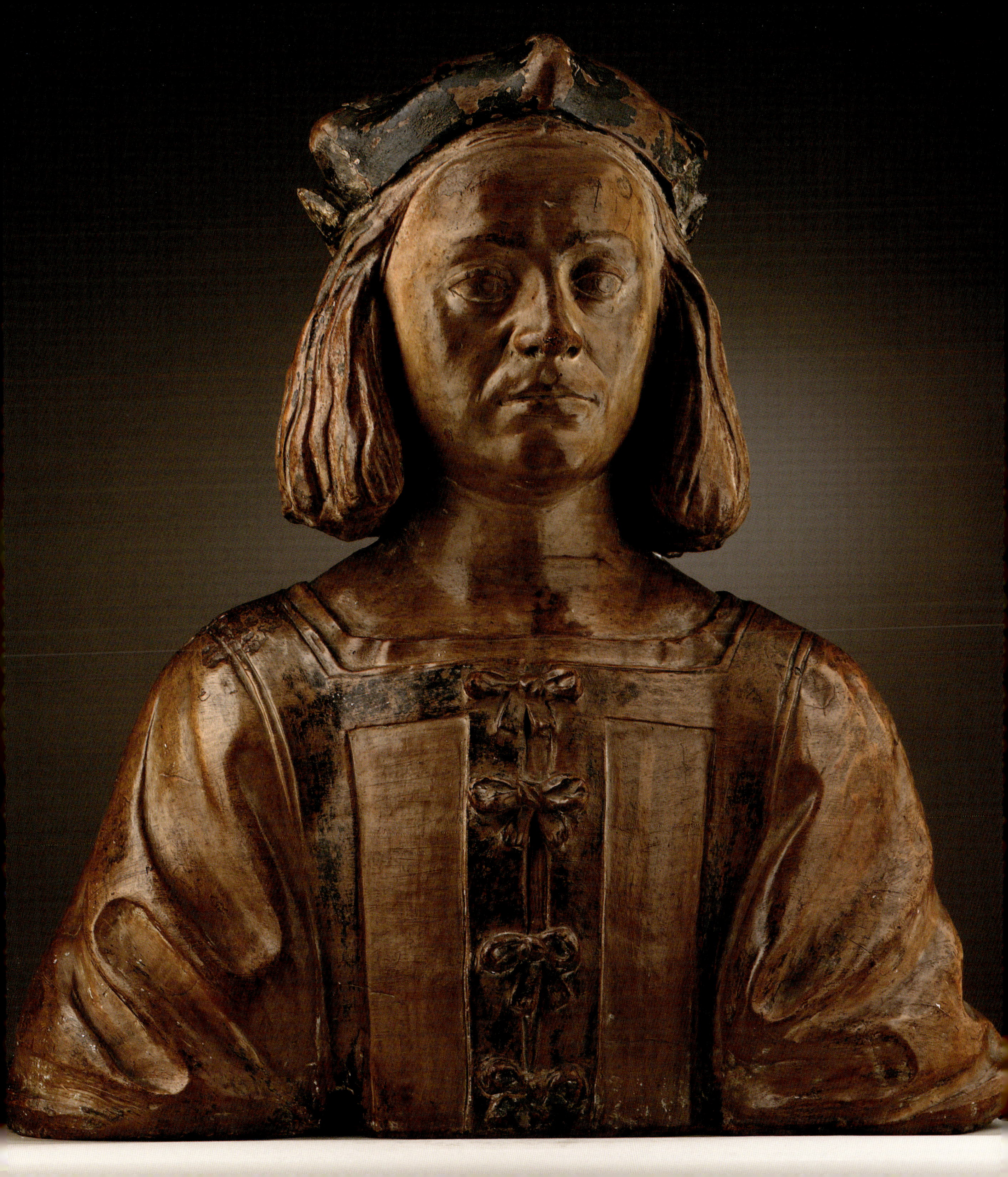

7. FLORENTINE, third quarter of the 16th century

(attributed to) (GIOVAN) BATTISTA LORENZI (1527–post-1594)

Alexander the Great as Jupiter Ammon

Marble relief

24 3/8 in. (62 cm) high, 18 7/8 in. (48 cm) wide

The subject of this unpublished marble oval medallion may be identified by comparison with ancient coinage as Alexander the Great. The strong projection of his forehead over the brow is a distinguishing feature. The short ram's horn visible amidst the hair over his temple identifies Alexander in the persona of Jupiter Ammon, under which name the ruler of the Olympian gods was worshipped in Egypt.

The practice of reproducing heads from ancient coins (for example of the first twelve Roman emperors) as large medallions for insertion in facing pairs or series within frames on walls – to lend an added air of antiquity to the architecture – was characteristic of the Italian Renaissance, established by Donatello, Desiderio da Settignano and Mino da Fiesole in Florence, about the middle of the Quattrocento, and pursued vigorously a century later by the Medici dukes. The author of the present 'new' medallion is therefore to be sought in their circle of court sculptors, which had at its head the towering figure of Baccio Bandinelli. However, while the general appearance of this image of Alexander is similar to his many profile portraits in marble, it does not seem to be by his hand.

Its style is closest, among his followers, to that of Battista Lorenzi, who was even nicknamed, after Bandinelli's much-vaunted title of knight, as 'del Cavaliere'. Battista entered Bandinelli's workshop around 1540 and then collaborated with Vincenzo de' Rossi in Rome (1558–59). In 1564, the year of Michelangelo's death, Battista was elected to the newly formed Academy of Design in Florence and allocated the carving of one of three allegorical statues of the arts for the great master's tomb in Santa Croce, as well as the portrait-bust, a mark of the esteem in which he was held. Four years later Alamanno Bandini commissioned from him a group of *Alpheus and Arethusa* (now in the Metropolitan Museum of Art, New York), and it is with the profile of the head of *Alpheus* that the present work may best be compared, with its knitted brow, strong aquiline nose and projecting chin. An obvious technical feature of the Alexander, the drill-marks that are left unashamedly between the locks of hair, in order to create the effect of deep, but soft, shadow, is also to be found in the fountain figure, though its sharpness has been dulled by the effects of weathering.

In the archives of the Salviati family in Pisa there is a series of payments from 1573 to 1580 to Battista for the highly skilled job of restoring antique statues, which is sufficient proof of his close familiarity with the art of the ancient world. In the Opera del Primaziale of Pisa there is a bust of Hadrian, after the antique, which is now given to Battista (Pratesi 2003, pl. 559). Battista was thus pre-eminently qualified to carve a portrait-relief such as the present one, showing one of the major figures of ancient history. C.A.

RELATED LITERATURE

A. Bostrom, 'Battista Lorenzi', in J. Turner, ed., *The Dictionary of Art*, London and New York 1996, XIX, p. 672

C. del Bravo in *Il 'Ganimede' di Battista Lorenzi: il restauro di un'opera di un settignanese*, exh. cat., Misericordia di Settignano, Florence, 30 October–19 December 1982, pp. 11–31

G. Pratesi, ed., *Repertorio della scultura fiorentina del Cinquecento*, Turin 2003, vol. III, pl. 559

P. Remington, 'Alpheus and Arethusa: A Marble Group by Battista Lorenzi', *Bulletin of the Metropolitan Museum of Art, New York*, 1940, pp. 61–65

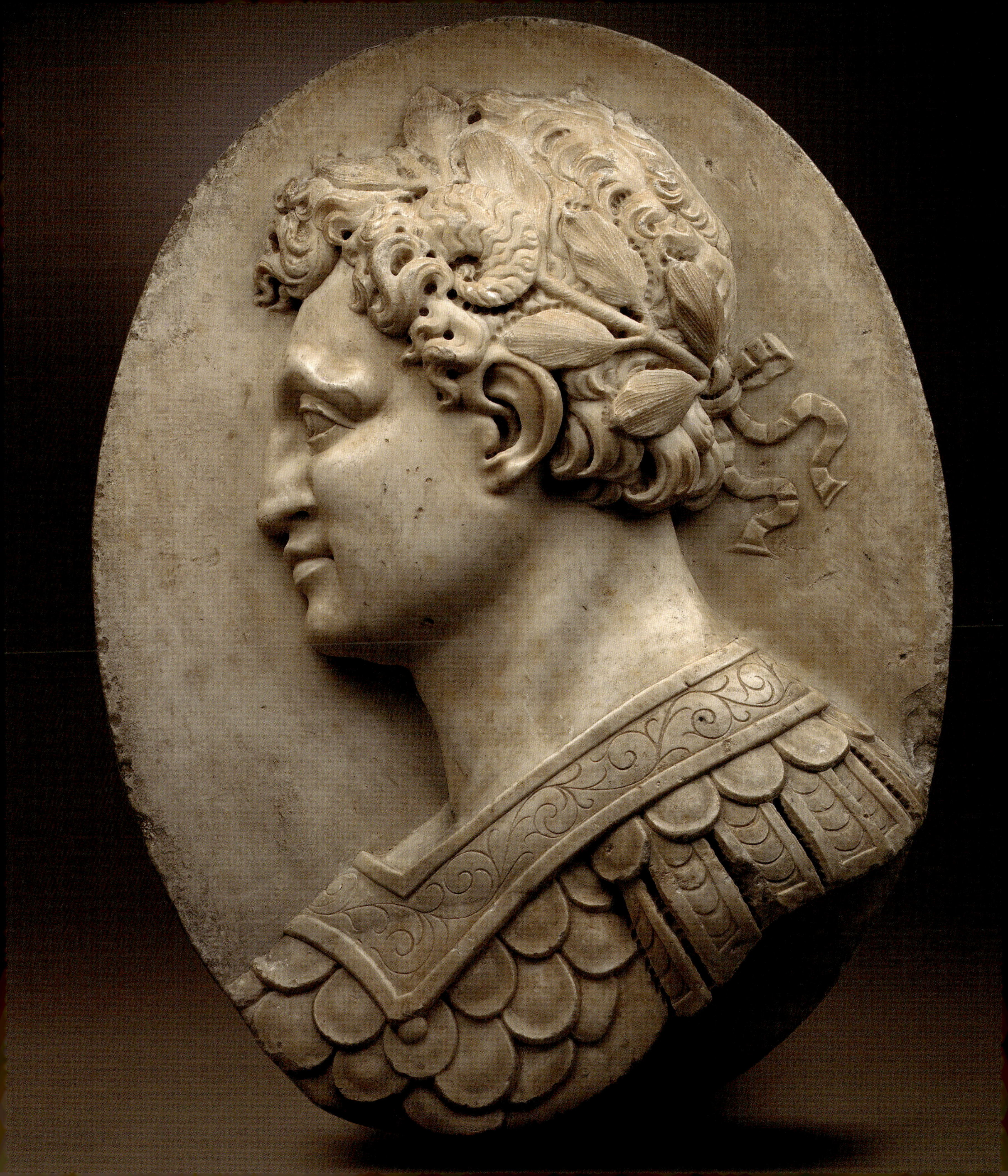

8. ROMAN, late 16th century

Cast from [lost] models of *c.* 1550 attributed to

MICHELANGELO BUONARROTI (1475–1564)

The Good and the Bad Thieves, from the Crucifixion

Bronze, reddish-brown patina

The Good Thief: 10 in. (25.5 cm) high, 10 1/4 in. (26 cm) wide
The Bad Thief: 9 7/8 in. (25 cm) high, 10 1/4 in. (26 cm) wide

These statuettes are components of what would have been a symmetrically disposed group of three figures depicting *The Crucifixion of Christ*, as recorded in the Gospel of St Luke (24: 32–33; 39–43)

One statuette shows the *Bad Thief*, averting his head from Christ and turning it sharply to his left (the 'sinister' side) and downwards (notionally, in the direction of Hell); he tugs away from his right arm, so that his left one is slightly relaxed and his thorax is rotated in the same direction, though from the waist down his torso remains frontal. He also pushes himself away from the cross to which he is nailed with his sharply bent left leg. Meanwhile, the *Good Thief* presses upwards, bracing his arms against the cross, and raising his face urgently towards the Saviour as he addresses him.

The Christ (missing here) is shown frontally, with his head bowed forward and his body positioned symmetrically about the axis of the cross, and his feet crossed and nailed separately. There is no trace of the physical torture of the crucifixion or the psychological and spiritual agony experienced by Christ. Michelangelo, who is believed to be the author of these figures and was a deeply religious man, must have conceived the central image as a beatific vision of Christ, as Salvator Mundi, transcending earthly things as represented by the flanking figures of thieves.

Michelangelo was involved with the image of Christ crucified at three points in his career: first, according to Vasari, he made a wooden crucifix in gratitude to the monk at Santo Spirito who had let him make dissections of corpses awaiting burial there in order to perfect his knowledge of anatomy (this may – or may not! – be identical to the slim, wooden figure of near life-size now in the Casa Buonarotti); secondly, in the 1540s he tackled the theme of the Crucifixion under the influence of Vittoria Colonna, which resulted in a fairly muscular image of Christ, with his head raised and his body posed in strong *contrapposto*; and thirdly, towards the end of his life, after Vittoria's death in 1547, he arrived at the concept of a frontal nude Christ hanging more or less symmetrically on the cross, for which there are several drawings in the Louvre.

It was at this stage that he wrote despairingly in a sonnet:

Né pinger né scolpir fie più che quieti
L'anima, volta a quell'amor divino
C'aperse a prender noi 'n croce le braccia

(Neither painting nor sculpture is any longer capable of calming the soul, turned to that divine love which opens its arms upon the cross to receive us).

A bronze group of three crucified figures, including the two thieves of which these are rare casts of top quality, first appeared in the sales at Christie's of the noted Florentine antique dealer Stefano Bardini in 1899 (London) and again in 1918 (New York), where it was bought by a private collector, from whose hands it reached the Metropolitan Museum of Art, New York, in 1937 (inv. no. 37.28, A.D. Rogers Fund). Wilhelm von Bode

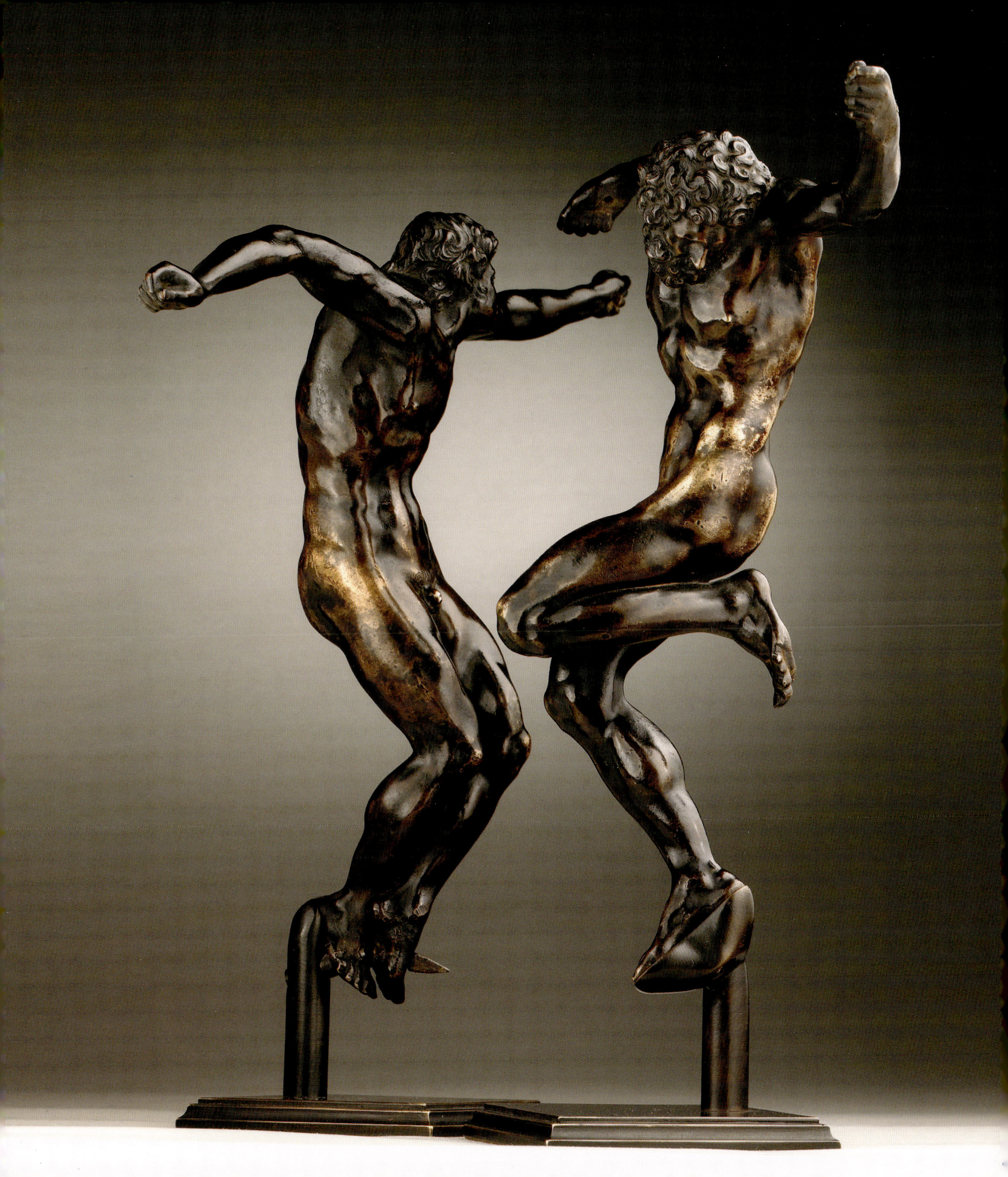

mentioned this as a "free copy" (*freie Nachbildung*) in his writings about bronze statuettes (1908; 1930).

Mr Phillips, then curator, wrote of it: "A handsome and apparently unique bronze group … which may well be a close copy of sculptures that he modelled. Much evidence concerning our figure of Christ … suggests that our group is closely connected with the work of Michelangelo. In 1597, only a little more than thirty years after the death of Michelangelo, the Spanish silversmith Juan Baptista Franconio brought from Rome to Seville a small crucifix, which, according to to Francisco Pacheco (1564–1654), was even then ascribed to the Florentine. Franconio's Christ, which Spanish artists of the day received with great enthusiasm, has since been lost, but it apparently was the original of several crucifixes cast in various metals now to be found in public and private collections in Spain. Gomez-Moreño has noted and illustrated a number of these, all of which are amazingly like the central figure from our Crucifixion group."

A weak copy drawing in pen and ink of the *Bad Thief* now in the Teyler Museum, Haarlem, is helpfully labelled *Il Ladrone di Micel'Agnolo Buonarotti* (de Tolnay 1971, pp. 172–73, pl. 332). In any case, the strongly muscled and contorted bodies of the two thieves, demonstrating a mastery of *contrapposto*, corroborate the connection of the group with the hand of Michelangelo (de Tolnay 1971, pls. 329–30). Other good casts are in the Civiche Raccolte d'Arte Applicata ed Incisioni in the Castello Sforzesco, Milan. (Weak after-casts – *e.g.* Louvre, Gatteaux Bequest, 1881; Staatliche Museen, Berlin, inv. no. 2798, bought in Florence in 1904 – perhaps taken from Michelangelo's original, but by then deteriorating, wax models, show the same torso for the *Bad Thief*, but a different one – in mirror-image – for the *Good Thief*, though both are without the limbs, which give them a Rodinesque appearance. None has an 'old' provenance and they may indeed have been manufactured in the time of – or even by – Rodin.)

Statuettes such as these, closely reflecting models by Michelangelo, could have been produced by an assistant of his, a bronze-founder called Giacomo or Jacopo del Duca (*c.* 1520–1604), who made – allegedly from models left behind at Michelangelo's death (1564) – some reliefs of the *Passion of Christ* on a bronze tabernacle now in the Museo di Capodimonte, Naples. This may have been intended by Michelangelo for Santa Maria degli Angeli in Rome. The figure of Christ in the panel showing the *Crucifixion* is very close to the type of Christ normally found between the present type of thieves in respect of the use of four nails and crossed legs, though Del Duca decided it would be more decent to conceal Christ's loins with the normal loincloth. C.A.

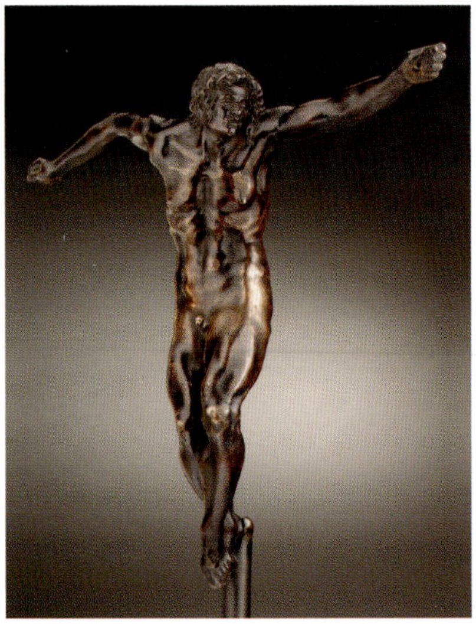

RELATED LITERATURE

J. Goldsmith Phillips, 'A Crucifixion group after Michelangelo', *Bulletin of the Metropolitan Museum of Art, New York*, XXXII, 9 September 1937, pp. 210–14

M. Gomez-Moreño, 'Obras de Miguel Angel en España', *Archivo español de arte y arqueologia*, VI, 1930, pp. 192–96; and IX, 1933, pp. 81–84

Musée national du Louvre, *Catalogue des bronzes et cuivres du moyen âge, de la Renaissance et des temps modernes*, Paris 1904, nos. 115–16

C. de Tolnay, *Michelangelo, V: The Final Period*, Princeton, New Jersey 1971, pp. 172–73, 221–25, 272–73, pls. 222–31, 327–28

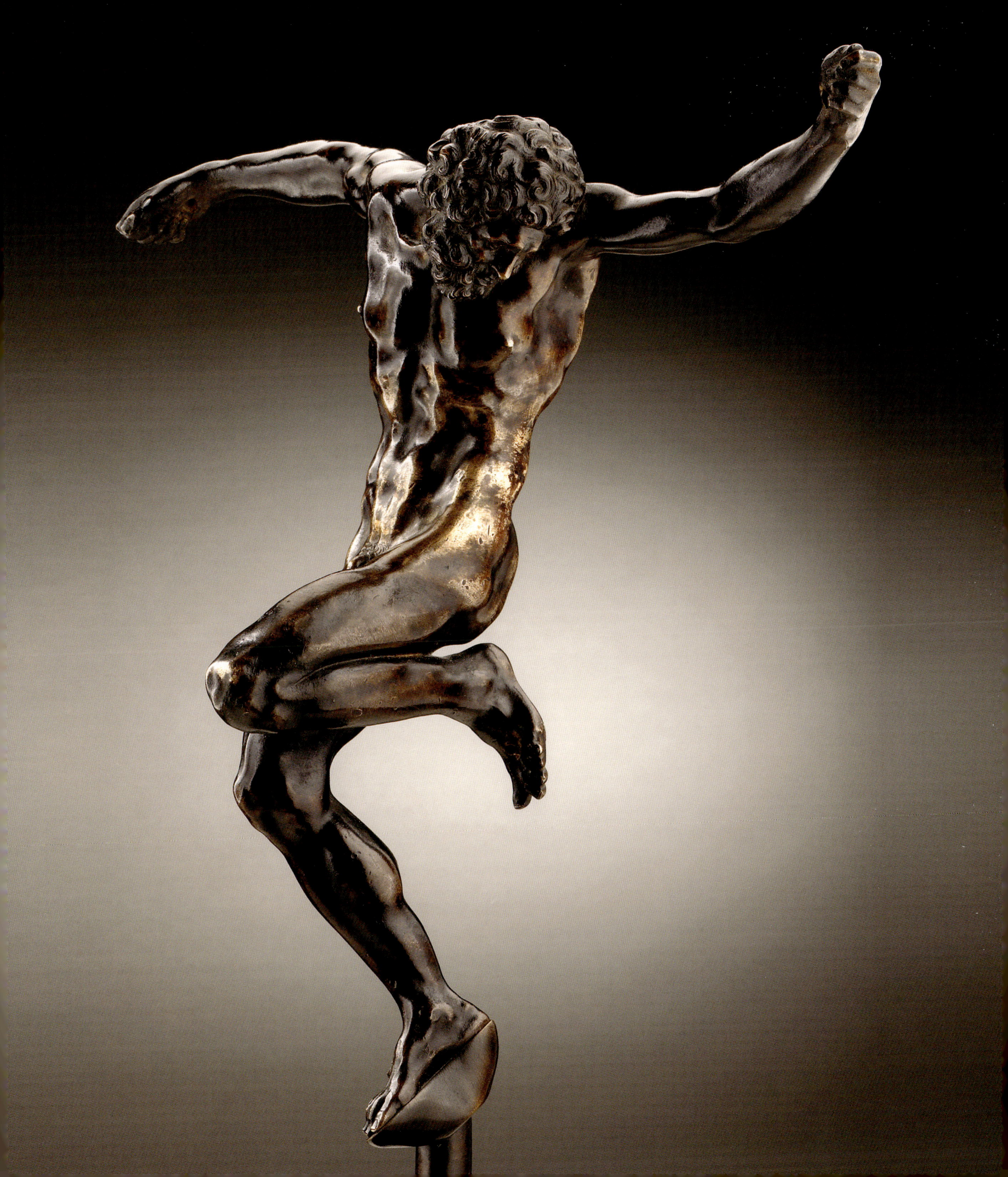

9. GIAMBOLOGNA (1529–1608)

Prometheus bringing Fire to Mankind

Gilt bronze

9 3/8 in. (23.7 cm) high

PROVENANCE: Comtesse de Chabannes, Château de la Bredé, near Bordeaux

Prometheus was a Greek demigod, one of the race of Titans. After the Great Flood he re-created mankind from clay and water (or with his own tears). He bore a silent grudge against Zeus (Jupiter) and the gods of Olympus for having destroyed the other Titans, and favoured mortals over them. Zeus, feeling cheated at the cunning way in which Prometheus had divided up the divine and mortal allocations of the sacrificial ox to favour the mortals, decided to withhold fire from them. Prometheus therefore stole a firebrand from the forge of Hephaestus (Vulcan) and, hiding it in a hollow stalk, took it down to earth. Whilst mankind benefited, Prometheus paid for his wiles by being chained to a rock and having his liver pecked at by an eagle for all eternity.

The statuette shows Prometheus performing his generous, but incautious, deed. Holding a classical torch (flames downward, perhaps for the sake of concealment from Zeus), he is stepping boldly forward across a terrain on which a vine is re-sprouting from an old root. The athletic, mature bearded male nude pauses in a *contrapposto* stance: his left shoulder and arm are advanced in front of the weight-bearing right leg, while his right shoulder is withdrawn and the arm is bent akimbo, thus counter-pointing the left leg, which trails behind as the pace is about to be completed, with only three of its toes still resting on the ground. The Titan, with his beetling brow and fine head of curly hair, looks pensively downward to his left as though assessing the plight of humankind, which he is about to ameliorate with his gift of fire.

When a newly discovered masterpiece emerges from obscurity, identifying the authorship can be problematic. In this case, however, it is a straightforward process, for the work bears all the hallmarks of Giambologna. Starting from first principles, the type of figure and its pose immediately recall those of a popular statuette by Giambologna, the so-called *Mars, Gladiator,* or *Executioner* (see illustration overleaf). The features that the two statuettes have in common are too many and too obvious to need enumerating. Clearly, though, from the elbows downward, the action of the arms and hands differ according to the subject.

The piling up of the curly forelock above the noble forehead, with the flanking bumps of curls projecting sideways and the 'walrus' moustache that all but conceals the lips above the temples, is even more pronounced in the case of Prometheus. This type of thickly bearded head is omnipresent in Giambologna's sculpture, not only in his monumental works but in the many panels of narrative relief that he produced mid-career for the Salviati Chapel in San Marco, Florence (1581–87) and for the Grimaldi Chapel in Genoa (*c.* 1585–87, now in the University).

Among the former series, one might single out the foremost onlooker at the left, who looks down towards the viewer and points back towards St Antoninus (Gibbons 1995, p. 42, fig. 32); or, among the latter series, the rabbis on horseback at the left upper corner of the scene showing *The Way to Calvary* (Gibbons 1995, p. 117, fig. 58b).

The profile of the face, when looking to the viewer's right, may also be compared with that of Hercules in the 'prototype' group, with a centaur, in Vienna, as may be the hand, with its pronounced, squared-off knuckles and fingernails (Gasparotto 2005, pp. 130–31).

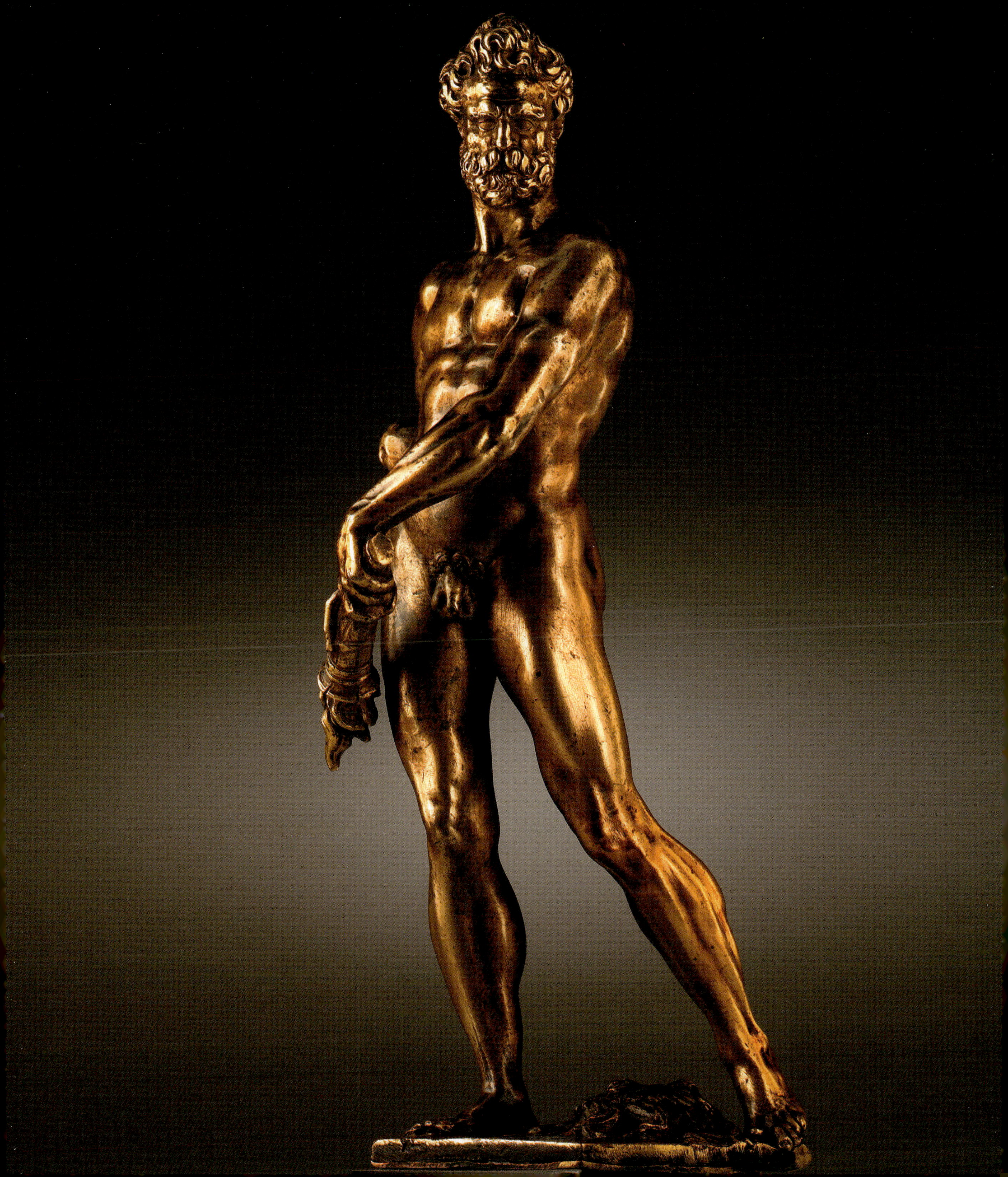

The design of Prometheus's left hand, with the fingers fanning out, though bent, under the extended index fingers, is, again, a motif beloved of Giambologna: it is to be found, for example, in the marble statues of *Neptune* (from the Fountain of Ocean, but now in the Bargello) and on *St Philip* (Gasparotto 2005, pp. 109, 153), to name but two.

Other features that the Prometheus shares with numerous documented pieces by Giambologna are the 'starfish' pattern of curls radiating from the crown of the head, the triangular shape of the navel and the large 'dimple' of contracted muscles on the hips and buttocks (for the hair, see a detail of a *Mars* in Seipel 2006, p. 225.).

While the subject of this figure does not appear among those listed among Giambologna's works by official documents or contemporary writers, nor do those of many other statuettes that are today universally held to be by him. The relatively small size and careful, though 'sculptural' (as opposed to goldsmith-like) finish, combined with the rarity of this cast, all suggest that it may have been created quite early in Giambologna's career, when he was only just beginning to work for the Medici. C.A.

COMPARATIVE LITERATURE

C. Avery, *Giambologna: The Complete Sculpture,* New York 1987
D. Gasparotto, *Giambologna* (I Grandi Scultori, no. 12), Rome 2005
M.W. Gibbons, *Giambologna: Narrator of the Catholic Reformation,* Berkeley 1995
W. Seipel, ed., *Giambologna: Triumph des Körpers,* exh. cat., Kunsthistorisches Museum, Vienna 2006

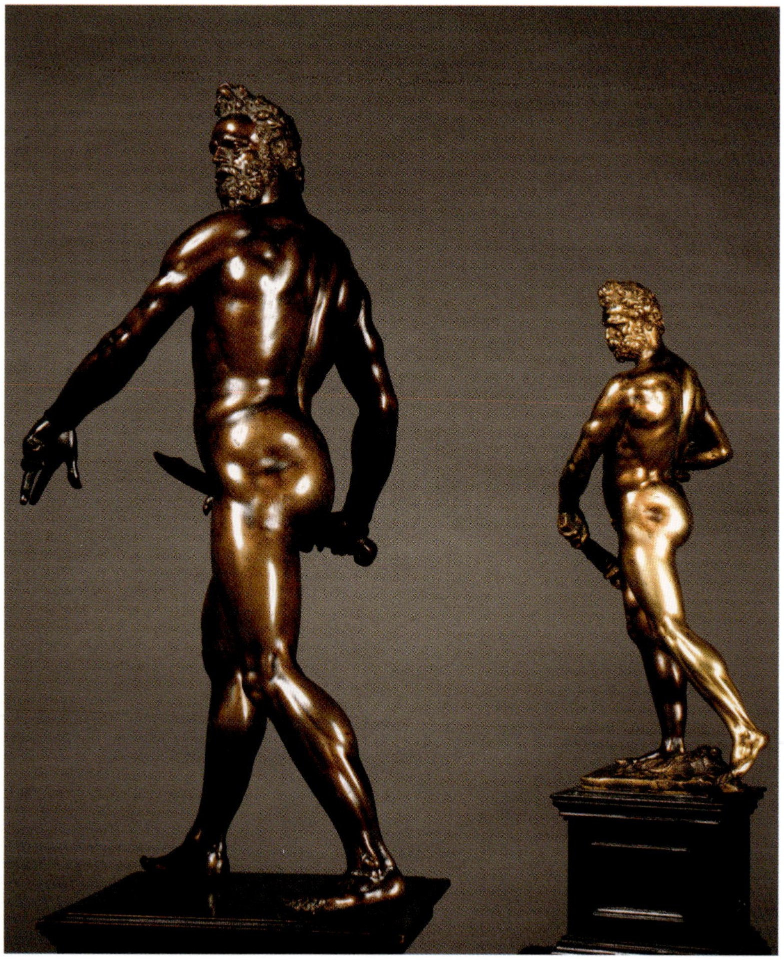

Fig. 1

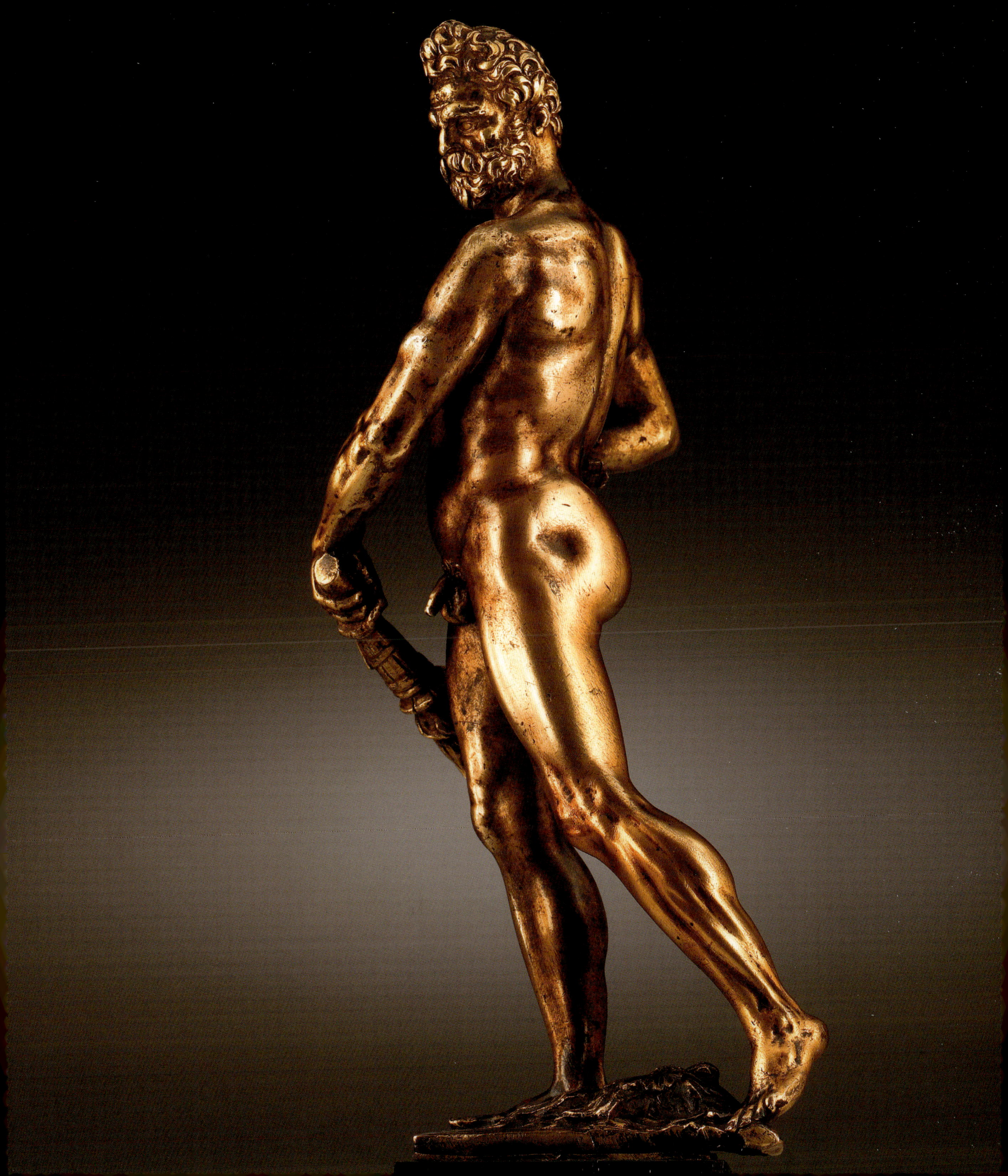

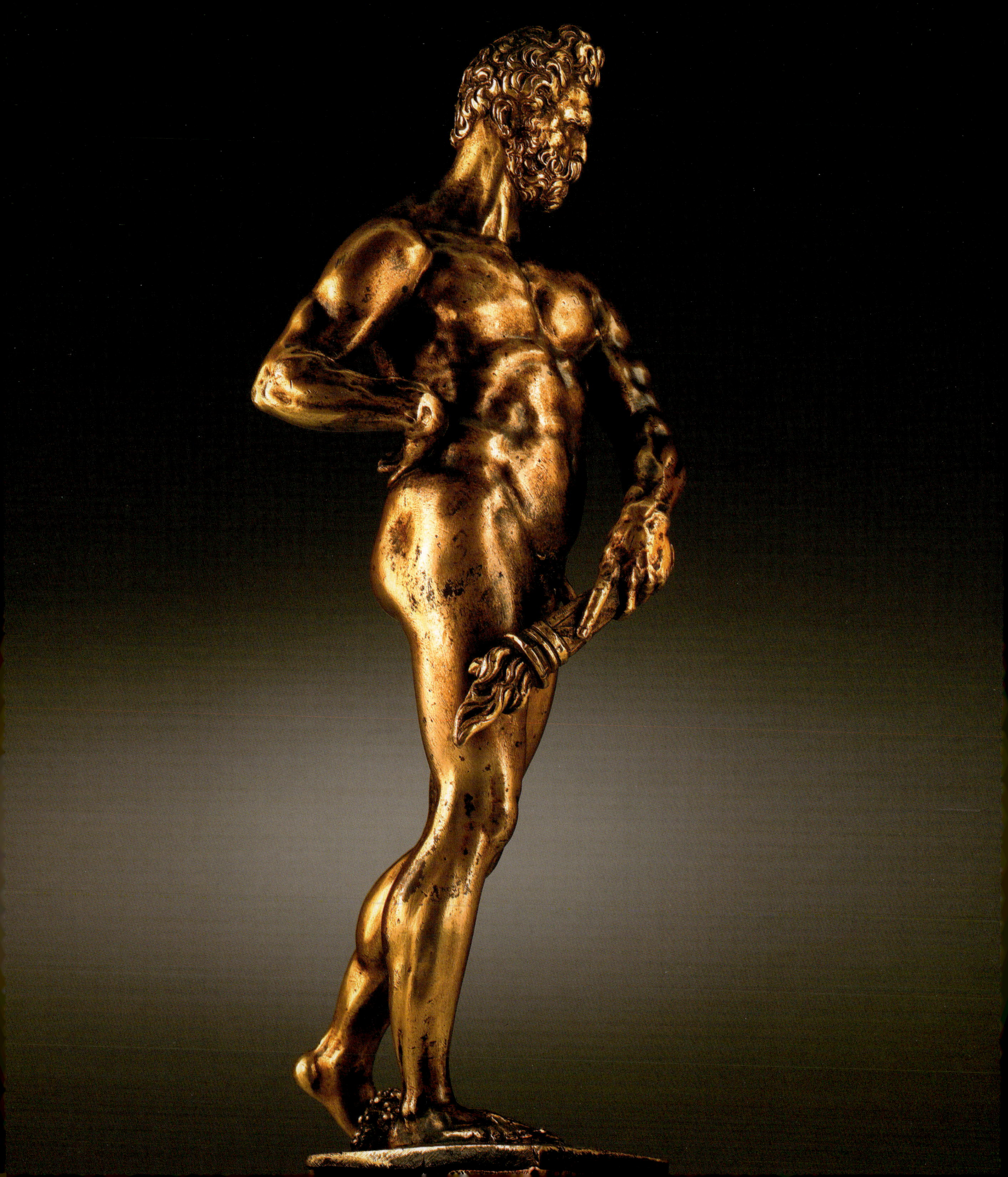

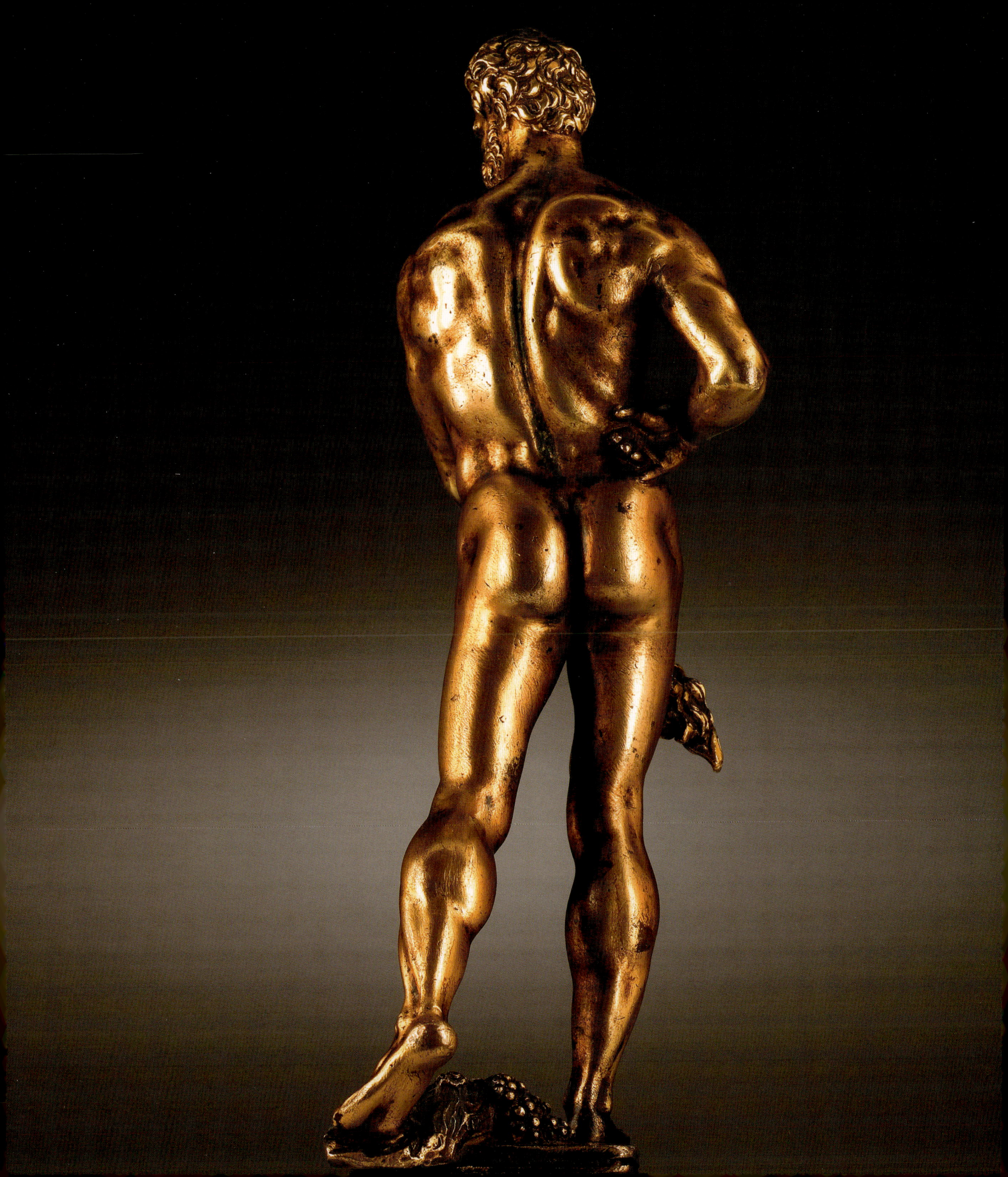

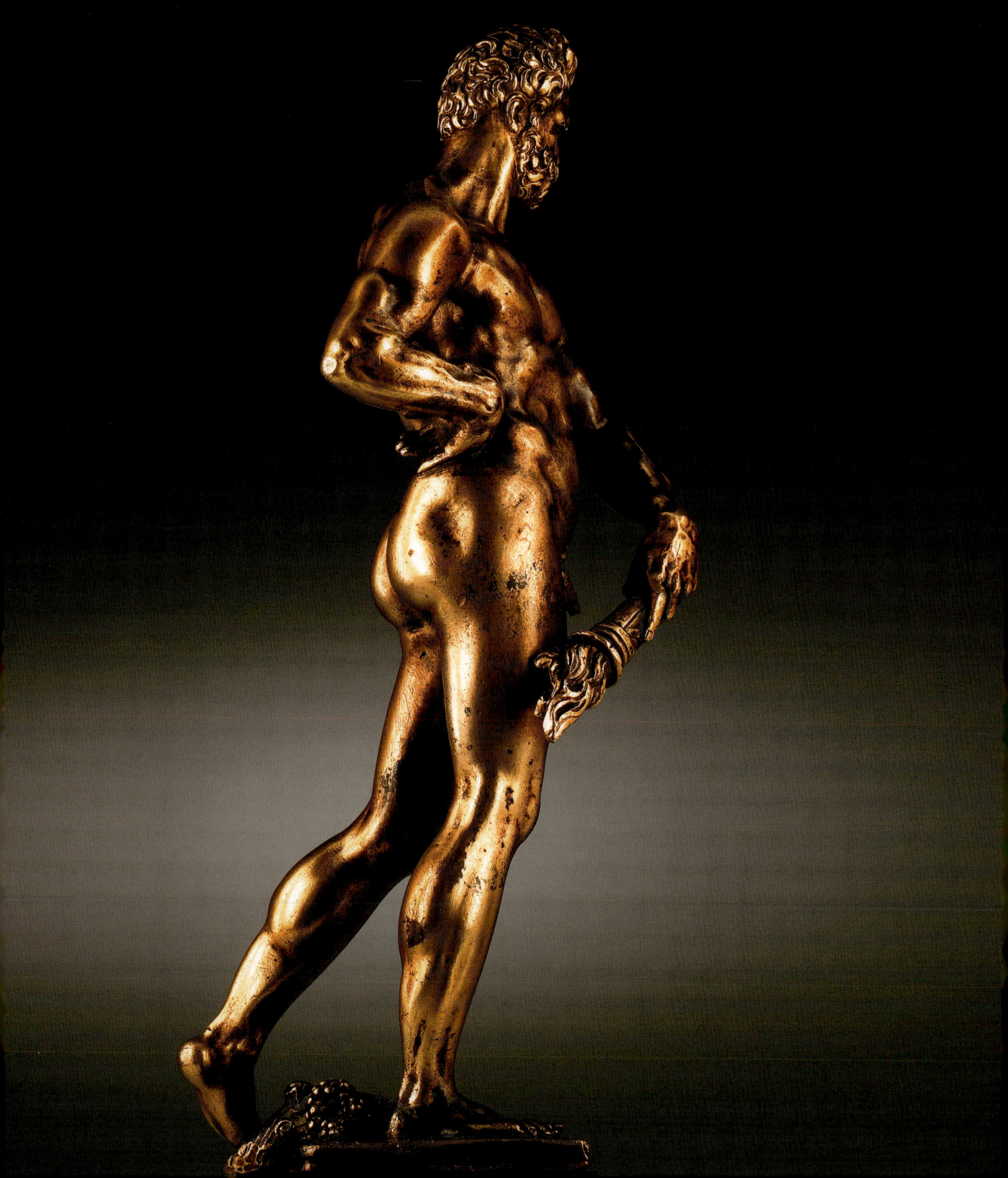

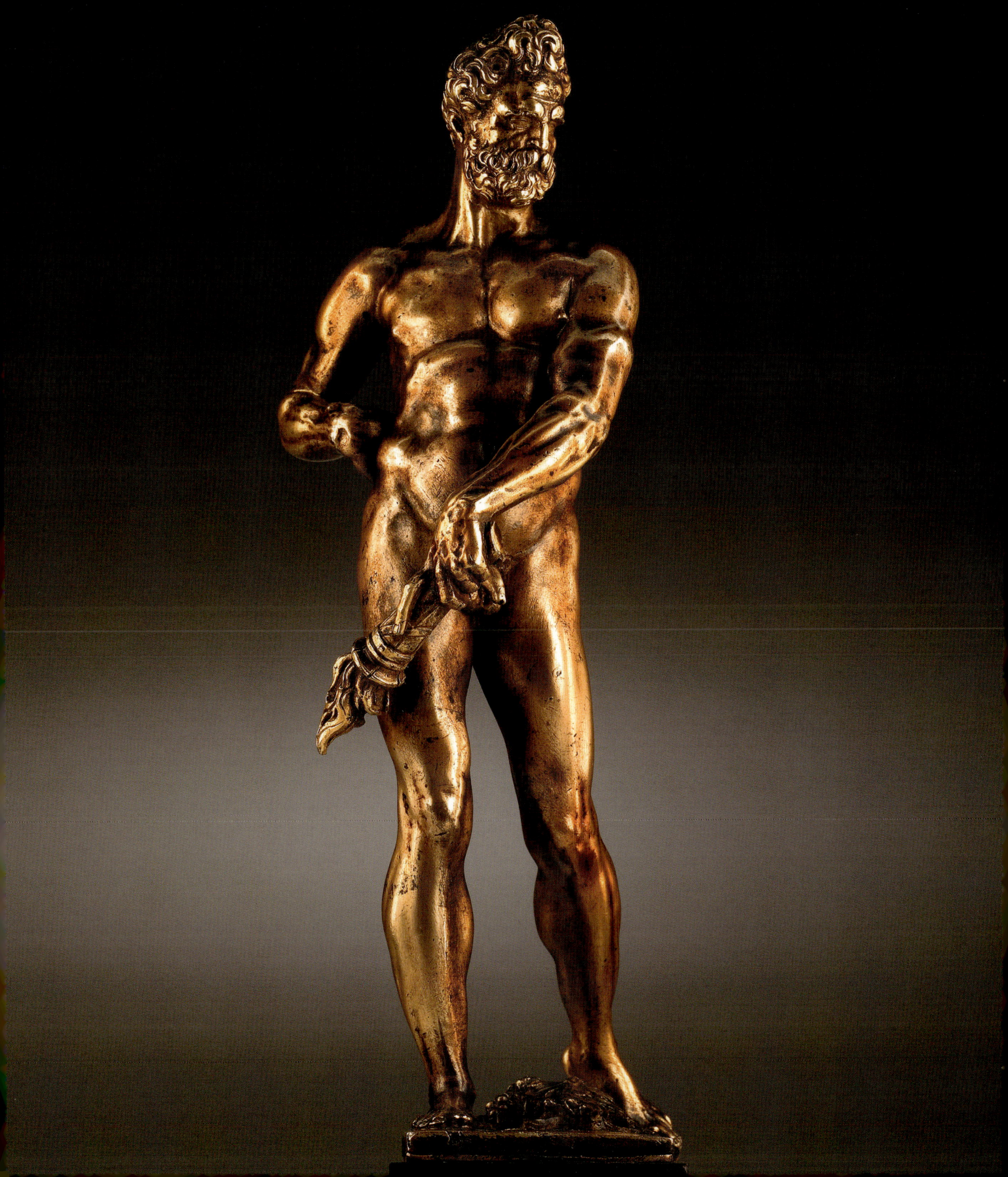

10. HUBERT GERHARD (*c.* 1550–1620)

Mounted River-god (Fountain Figure)

Munich or Augsburg, 1580s

Bronze

13 ½ in. (34.3 cm) high, 20 ½ in. (52 cm) wide

Direct cast; dark brown patina

PROVENANCE: Lady Kenmare; by descent to her son M. Cameron; private collection, South of France

This *River-god* has not appeared in the literature until now; it is without doubt an authentic work from the hand of Hubert Gerhard himself.

Along with Hans Mont, Pietro Francavilla, Adriaen de Vries and others, Gerhard was one of the young Dutch sculptors who left their hometown to hone their artistic skills in central Italy, particularly in Florence and Rome. Gerhard's initial training took place in Flanders and in 1581 there is evidence of his presence in the Medici court circle in Florence. Together with de Vries, he was one of the younger pupils of Giambologna, from whom he learned the technique of monumental bronze sculpture. After de Vries, Hubert Gerhard is viewed as the most important bronze sculptor north of the Alps of the generation after Giambologna.

In 1581 Gerhard went straight from Florence to southern Germany, where he was able to spend the rest of his life in great activity. Well advised by the Florentine stuccadore and sculptor Carlo di Cesare del Palagio, the noble Fugger family in Augsburg gave him the commission for the bronzes of a funerary altar for their cousin Christoph Fugger – two larger reliefs as well as figures of Prophets, angels and putti (Victoria and Albert Museum). One may deduce from the commission that Gerhard must have already made his mark in Italy with bronze sculptures of small to medium format. For Hans Fugger and his brother Marx, who managed the business of the trading house, Gerhard and Carlo in the following years created large cycles of terracotta sculptures – the monumental decorative figures of Schloss Kirchheim in Swabia and a row of *Apostles* for the funerary chapel of Marx Fugger in St. Ulrich und Afra in Augsburg.

While completing this work, the sculptor was taken into the service of the Bavarian Duke William V. In Munich the majority of Gerhard's time was spent on monumental bronzes, the *St Michael* on the façade of the Jesuit church (and the terracotta figures in its interior), fountains for the ducal residence and a number of figures for a planned tomb. Though in service of the court, Gerhard was also able to work for other employers. He created a fountain with over twenty bronze figures that was extremely famous in its time (1584–87) for the duke's younger brother, Ferdinand; the *Augustus* fountain for the city of Augsburg (1589–94); for Hans Fugger, the *Mars and Venus* fountain in the inner courtyard of Schloss Kirchheim, the truly monumental centrepiece of which is still extant (1590; Bayerisches Nationalmuseum, Munich); as well as smaller private bronzes, such as a flying *Mercury* for an Augsburg copper trader (*c.* 1590–94?; Bayerisches Nationalmuseum, Munich) and a *Neptune* in cabinet format.

Mounted water-gods are among Gerhard's frequent themes for large-scale works. Indeed, one could say that it was Gerhard who introduced the theme to the north from Italy. All of Gerhard's three large fountains possessed a broad fountain basin, on the edge of which river-gods were mounted, after the example of the Florentine *Neptune* fountain by

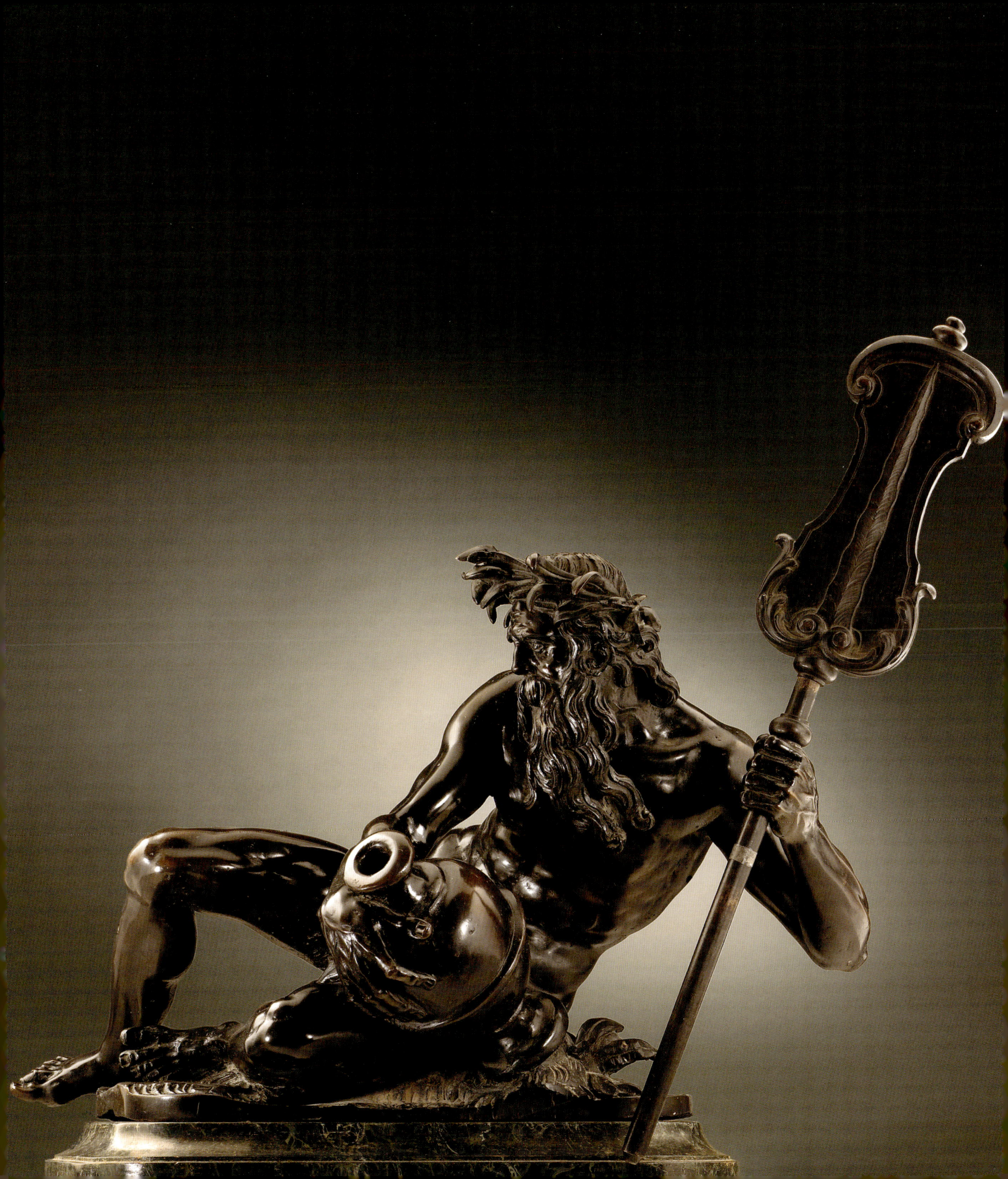

Ammannati's workshop. The Augsburg *Augustus* fountain is still situated in its original location, and the bronzes from an earlier Munich fountain have been redeployed in the so-called Wittelsbach fountain of the Munich Residenz; only the small-format figures of the fountain in Kirchheim, Swabia, have been lost. The Munich and Augsburg fountain figures offer the closest comparisons to the newly discovered *River-god*.

Following the abdication of Duke William V in 1597 and the dissolution of the essentially Italian, indeed Florentine-influenced Munich court workshops, Gerhard moved into service with the Habsburgs in Innsbruck. However, he received few commissions from Archduke Maximilian III, the Grand Master of the Teutonic Knights, and these were religious subjects without exception. Moreover, during the 1590s, when he faced a huge workload, a transformation came about in Gerhard's style: the powerful physicality of his figures, which, modelled in the face and body with deep shadows, often have a spontaneous effect, gave way to smoother, more attractively refined modelling. His later work shows less attention to detail, perhaps because the Florentine influence was waning, and he had little competition against which to work.

On stylistic grounds, despite the absence of archival sources, the newly discovered *River-god* can be said, without a doubt, to be an outstanding early work by Gerhard. In the complex, extensive composition of the body it is best compared to the Vienna *Mars and Venus* group, a collector's piece which, overturning opinions based on earlier research, is now held to be from Gerhard's early period. The direction of the *River-god*'s gaze contrasts with the opening of the upper body, and a third axis is created by the the urn flowing out towards the front. The contortion of the limbs gives the impression of a three-dimensionality that appears natural, and the composition is well thought out: his right leg and his left arm, with which he supports himself, form the rear and the lengthways extension of his body; the left leg, placed forward, and the right arm, which he uses to tip the urn, form the depthwise extension of the mounted figure.

The modelling of the individual parts – the face, in particular, and the hands and feet – are also best comparable to Gerhard's pieces from around 1580, to the *Prophets* of the Fugger altar as well as the four *River-gods* of the Wittelsbach fountain and the masculine river personification of the *Augustus* fountain. Characteristic are the ruffled beards, the veins protruding visibly on the backs of the hands, the feet and the neck, as well as the bulge of the knuckle-joints and the deeply chiselled, precisely delineated fingernails.

Particularly striking is the chasing of the face, which has been left rather rough, of the grainy strands of the beard and hair, with strong undercutting, and of the wreath of reeds. The powerful effect of light and shadow on these parts contrasts to the beautiful and smoothly chased epidermis of the body. All these techniques are also to be observed on the fountains. However, comparison with the *Mars and Venus* group, in which the faces have been chased more carefully, reveals that Gerhard also designed bronze sculpture in small format rather differently. The small Vienna bronze group was, from the outset, created for close viewing, indoors – as its brown varnish also demonstrates.

One can imagine the present figure as a garden fountain, in the open air, in an arbour or in a summer house – an idea borne out by the earthy base, with its grasses and plants, comparable to that of Ferdinand of Bavaria's fountain. As in Gerhard's other sculptures created to be seen in natural light, the *River-god* takes on an especially convincing three-dimensionality when seen lit from an angle and from above. Though the opening of the urn runs through the plinth, allowing for a water pipe to be easily installed, it is not possible to determine whether this fountain figure ever actually channelled water. If it did, it can only have been for a short period, for there are no traces in the patina of calcification having ever occurred.

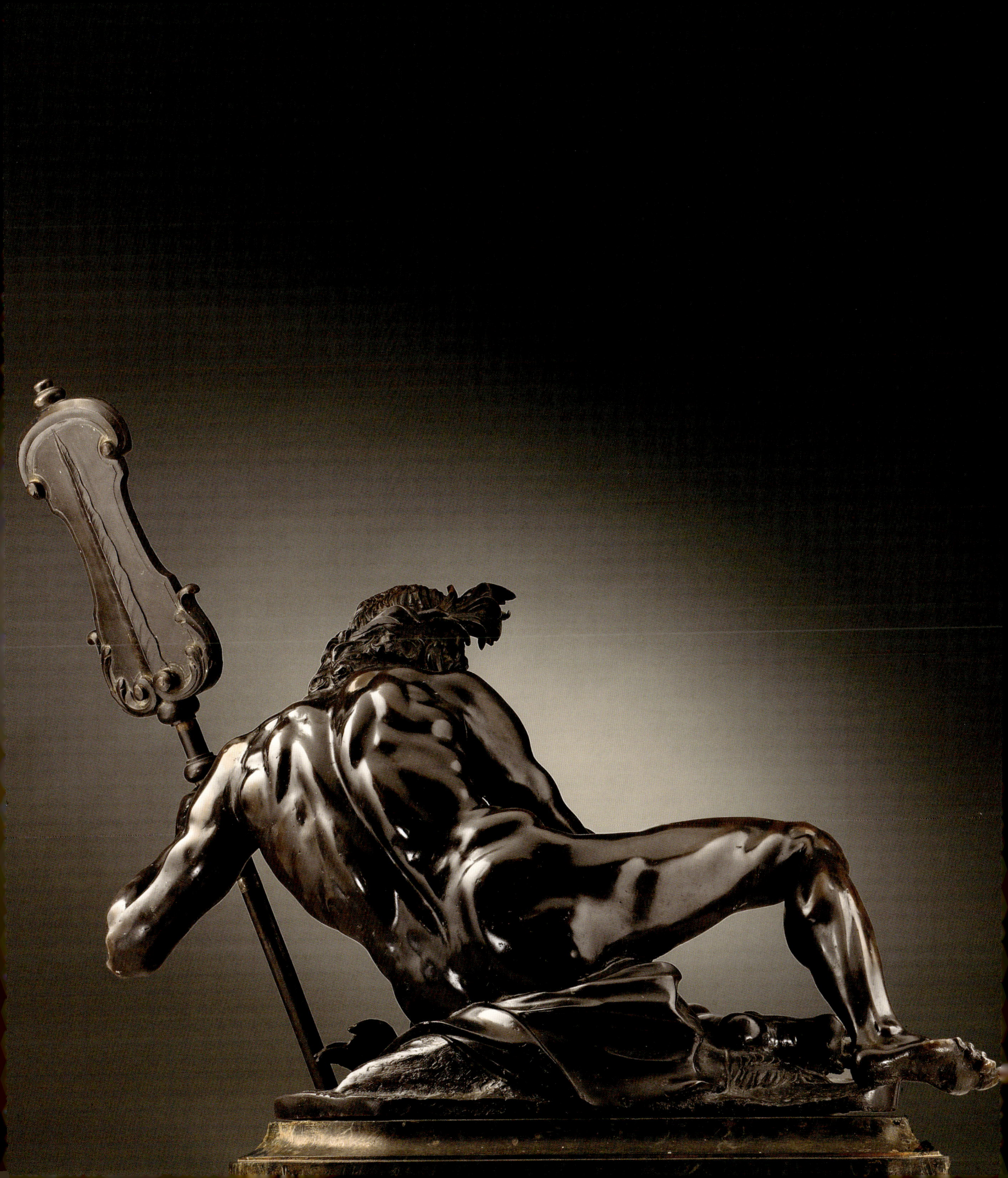

The *River-god* supports the whole weight of his upper body on the object on his left, a paddle or oar. Like other such personifications of the time, including Gerhard's *River Lech* on his *Augustus* fountain, he would have held the blade downwards. Whether the paddle itself is the original or a later replacement requires, in my opinion, further research. It might also be possible to reconstruct a trident in the *River-god* 's hand, although there is nothing to indicate that Neptune is intended here. In both his *Neptune* figures thus far known Gerhard did without attributes. In any case, it can be imagined that below the base-plate of the *River-god* there was firm ground or a plinth, on which he could support himself firmly with this shaft. Gerhard's figures rarely include anything unstable or suspended; on the contrary, they are rendered anatomically convincing by their fixed position. This awareness of the weight of the body, among other things, differentiates Gerhard's style from that of other successors of Giambologna.

The rounded, irregular triangular shape of the base-plate gives no indication of its original placement; nor are there any screw holes. However one imagines the *River-god* in his surroundings, whether free-standing, on the edge of a basin or occupying a niche, one may also imagine one or more counterparts. If one takes the front finishing edge of the base-plate as a 'main view', the powerful opening on one side would perhaps have required a visual counterbalance.

We know just as little about who commissioned Gerhard's river god as we do about its original placement. If we presume that it originated during Gerhard's earlier years in Germany, it seems likely that the patron was a figure from the Bavarian court or the Fugger family.

Immediately after Gerhard's arrival in Munich, and before his death in 1608, Ferdinand had the fountain already mentioned built in front of his palace, which lay in the centre of the city. Thanks to the opulence of its 150 water jets and the Olympic and river-gods mounted or standing about its edge, the fountain – the first of its kind in the north, in the Florentine style – drew attention from far and wide. Ferdinand was clearly the promoter of bronze sculpture *sur place*, a theme which reached a high point at the Munich court even before other courts, such as that of the Emperor, followed its lead. It was reported in Munich that Ferdinand himself worked in the casting workshop. In front of the city wall lay his extensive gardens, a description of which was given by the Augsburg art agent Philipp Hainhofer during his lifetime. Streams flowed through the gardens and there were five summerhouses filled with paintings. In one, according to Hainhofer, there was a bath and fountain with bronze figures and fifty water outflows (Diemer 2004, II, p. 135); this was almost certainly by Gerhard.

It was customary for people of high standing in the court to engage the services of the court sculptor. Thus, Landhofmeister (steward) Ottheinrich von Schwarzenberg (†1590) not only had obtained bronzes for his Munich funerary chapel from Gerhard, but also his portrait bust. Though we know nothing about the features of Schwarzenberg's garden, garden fountains had become commonplace in these circles. The duke's personal physician also engaged Gerhard's services, and we know of a *Pietà* for his private chapel.

It is conceivable that alongside their large commissions from Florentine sculptors, the Fuggers ordered smaller, private works for the interiors of their Augsburg residence and for the courts and gardens at Schloss Kirchheim. We know that near Augsburg there were Fugger gardens in which there was a bronze fountain by Hans Reisinger. All this has been lost, presumably transformed into money during the Thirty Years War, just as Schloss Kirchheim was stripped of its works of art, and an attempt was even made to sell the giant fountain group to Sweden.

Until now we have only known of authentic Gerhard bronzes in small or medium format; in this respect the discovery of the *River-god* represents a significant addition to his

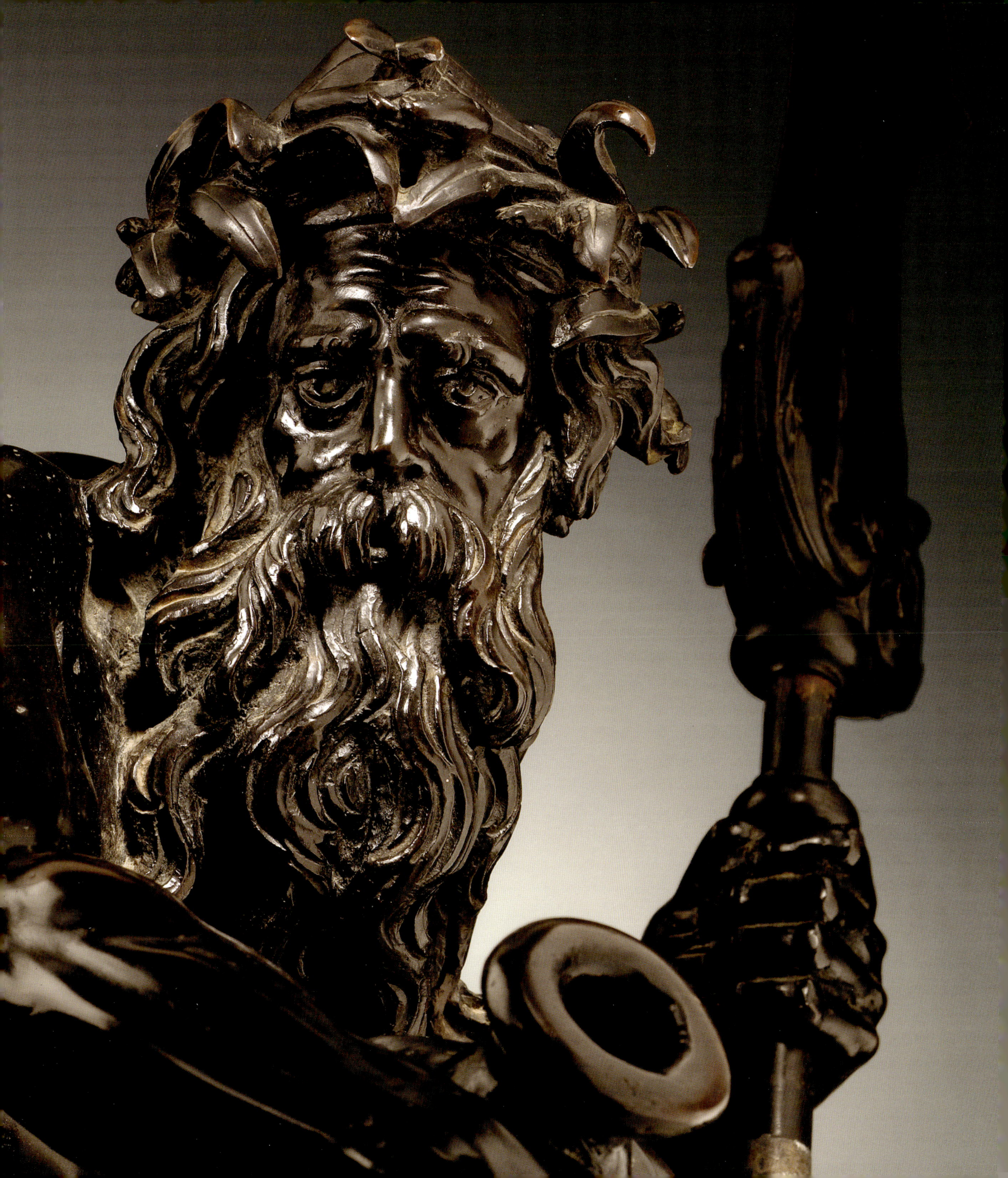

oeuvre and to its reconstruction. The Munich court's stock of small bronzes was completely destroyed in a fire in the eighteenth century. We therefore know three mythological groups in Gerhard's style only in very coarse later recasts. A *Water-nymph* (Detroit) no longer shows Gerhard's detailed spontaneous modelling, and is an indirect cast which may not be contemporaneous. The number of lost small bronzes should not be underestimated. D.D.

RELATED LITERATURE

D. Diemer, *Hubert Gerhard und Carlo di Cesare del Palagio. Bronzeplastiker der Spätrenaissance*, 2 vols., Berlin 2004
'Une maison palladienne sur la Côte d'Azur', *Connaissance des Arts,* no. 29, 15 July 1954, pp. 22–29, repr. p. 22

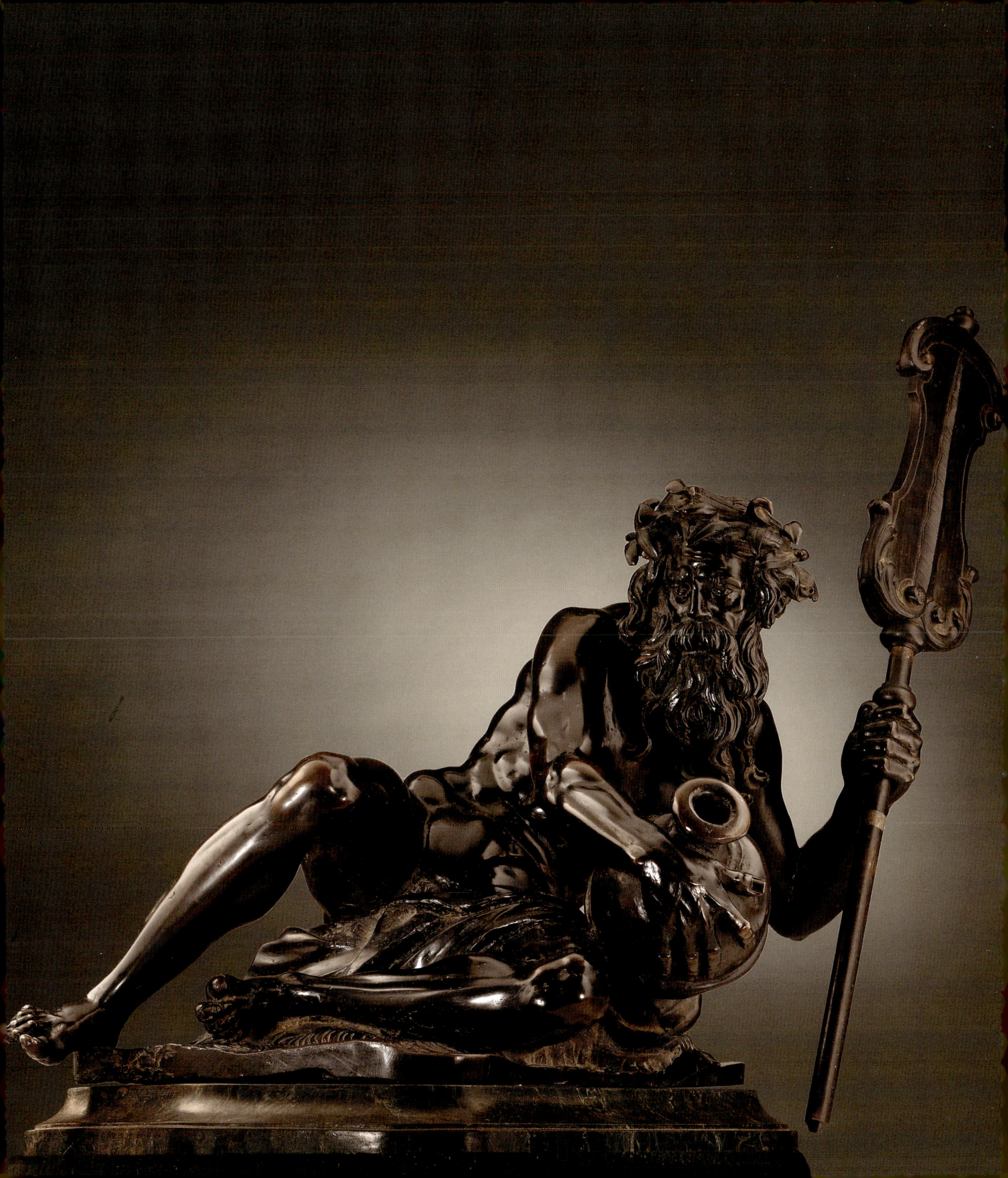

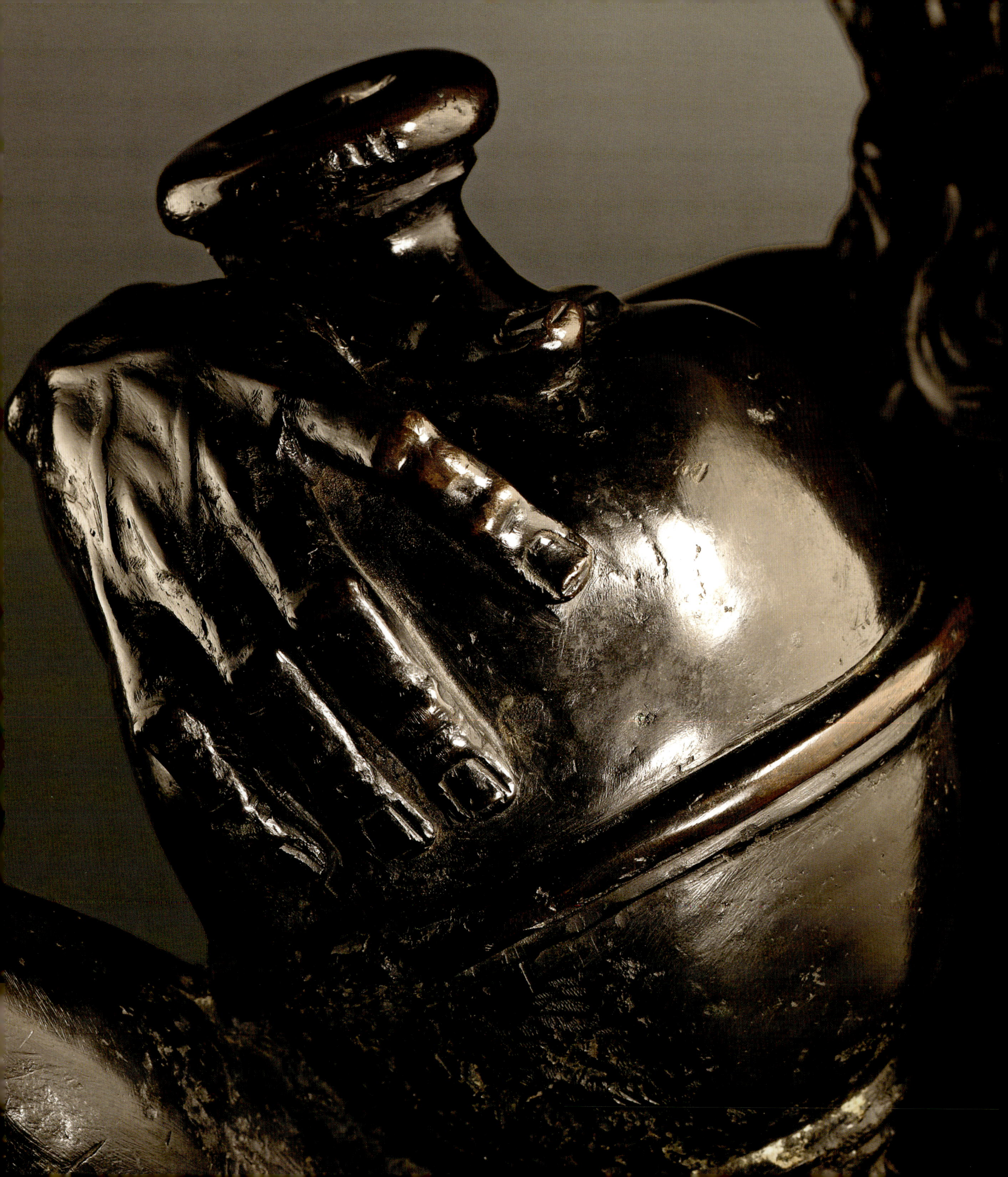

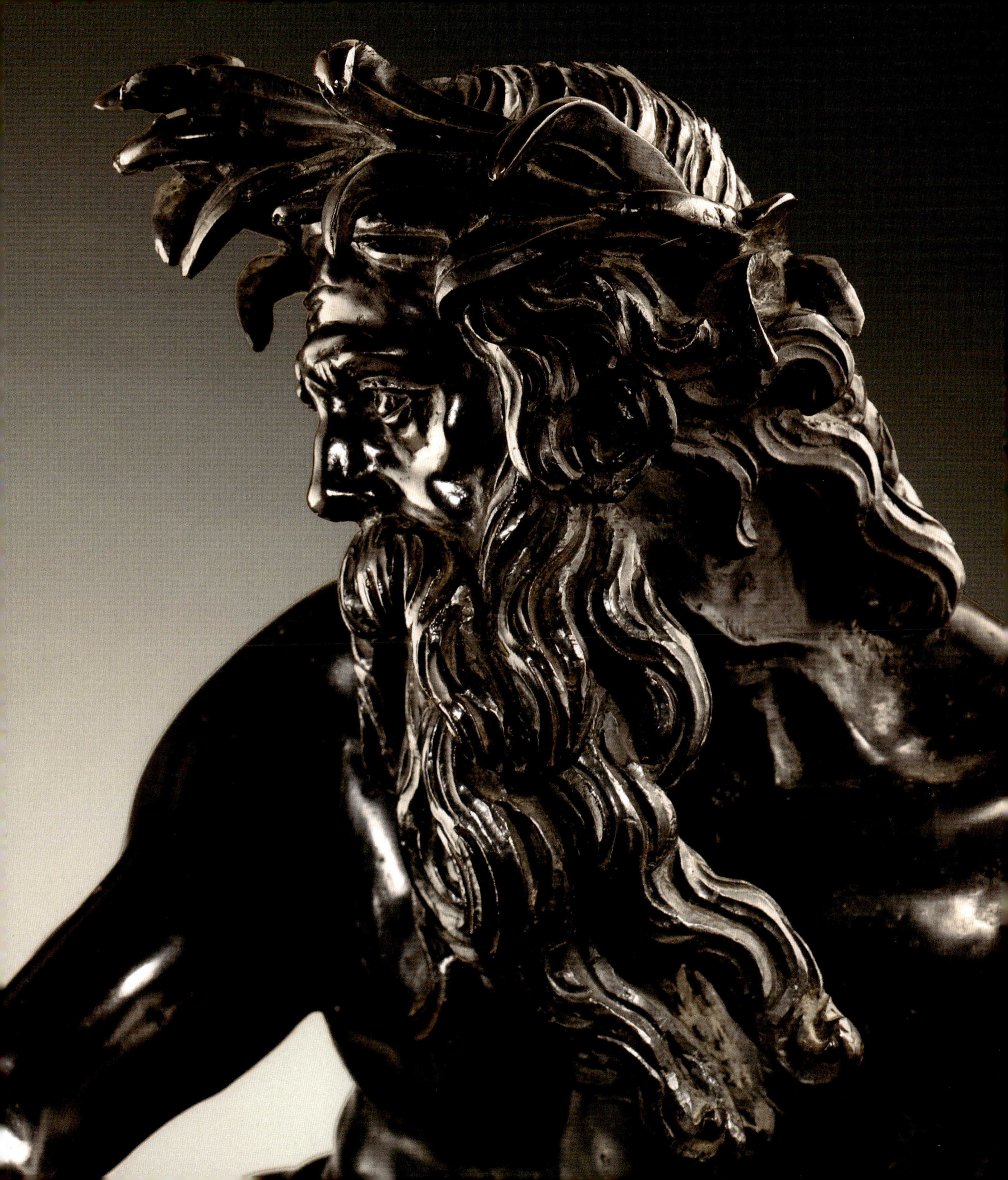

11. BARTHÉLEMY PRIEUR (*c.* 1536–1611)

Hercules slaying the Nemean Lion

Bronze, rich brown patina with extensive traces of red lacquer

7 in. (17.8 cm) high

PROVENANCE: Wadsworth Athenaeum

Barthélemy Prieur, like many other great sculptors from north of the Alps, was drawn to the Italian peninsula to further his studies of sculpture. It is known that he was in Rome as early as the 1550s, presumably having finished his initial training in France. From 1564 to 1567 he was employed as court sculptor to Duke Emanuel Philibert of Savoy, and after this appointment had come to an end he returned to Paris in 1571. Prieur was already making small-scale bronzes in the 1570s and 1580s, a fact recorded in the inventory drawn up on the death of his first wife in 1583. King Henri IV is known to have taken a liking to Prieur's smaller bronzes, which is probably why the artist began working for him from 1594 in Paris, where he spent the remainder of his career.

The quality of the cast and chiselling, along with the extremely fine colour and condition of the bronze, allows us to place this bronze in the highest milieu of Prieur's small-scale works. It also depicts a rare subject-matter, one which tests his artistic and technical abilities. Prieur has successfully rendered a large-scale subject on an intimate scale and has captured a heightened sense of tension and power, as the muscular body of Hercules prises open the jaws of the wild beast. Although the form is quite clearly Mannerist, it is evident that Prieur's early years spent in Rome armed him with an extensive understanding and knowledge of ancient sculpture, which is formatively expressed in our bronze.

RELATED LITERATURE

G. Brière and M. Lamy, 'L' Inventaire de Barthélemy Prieur, sculpteur du Roi', *Bulletin de la Société française de philosophie*, XCVI–XCII, April–June 1949, pp. 41–68

R. Seelig-Teuwen, *Barthélemy Prieur (1536–61),* PhD thesis, Ludwig Maximilian University of Munich, 1973

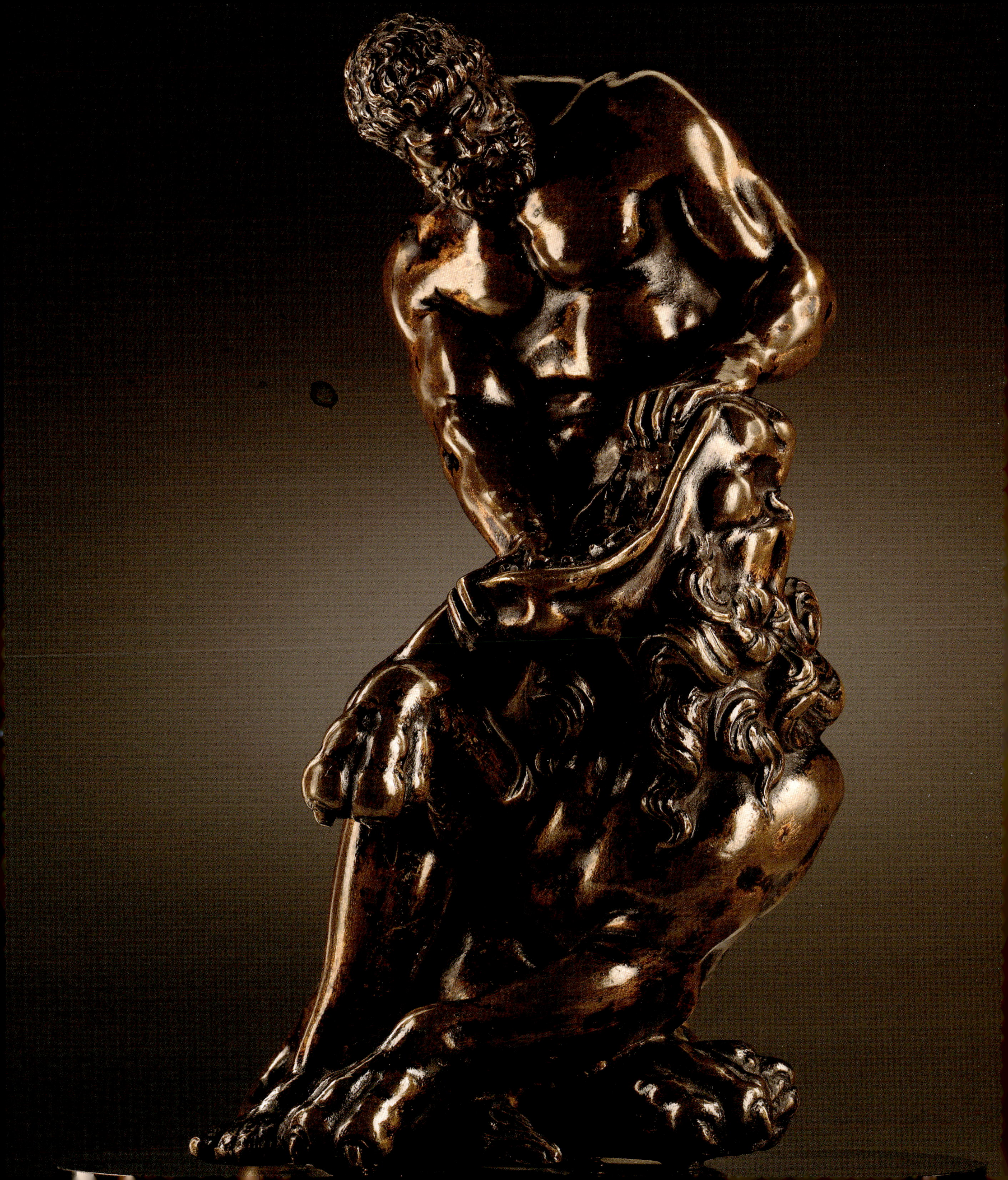

12. HUBERT LE SUEUR (active 1596–1658)

A General on Horseback

Bronze, rich brown patina

8 ½ in. (21.5 cm) high

This unpublished statuette is an interesting addition to the growing catalogue of work by Hubert Le Sueur, court sculptor – as he himself boasted – to two kings, Louis XIII of France and Charles I of England and Scotland. Unfortunately, it has no meaningful provenance and the identity of the armoured rider is unknown.

The horse, the saddle and the armoured body are identical to those of two other casts which have the heads of King Louis XIII as a youth and of King Philip of Spain, both now in the Victoria and Albert Museum, London, nos. A.1–1994 and A.108-1956. Of these, the former has Le Sueur's name stamped on the girth, and this was crucial for establishing his authorship not just of these small equestrian figures, but of a much larger pair also in the Victoria and Albert Museum (inv. nos. A. 47 and A 49–1951). One of the latter shows Louis XIII on a virtually identical mount, though the larger scale has permitted more modelling of detail. There is also a bronze of Charles I on a steed leaping above a crouching, defeated foe, which has come to light more recently (inv. no. A.1–1992; see Bresc-Bautier and Scherf 2009, pp. 176–77, no. 44, with earlier literature).

The tail and spare facial features, with close-cropped hair, to some extent recall those of Donatello's monument to the mercenary leader Il Gattamelata in Padua, of the 1450s. While this may be fortuitous, a connection between the Caroline court circle (for which Le Sueur worked) and Padua exists in the person of the art-loving Earl of Arundel, who died in exile there and is buried in the cloister of the Basilica of the Santo. He, or a relative in England, or indeed some other courtier who had enrolled in the famous University of Padua, might on his return home have commissioned Le Sueur to produce a small version. This would necessarily have been at arm's length, for the sculptor never went to Italy, and this would account for the discrepancies with the original.

On the other hand, the equestrian subject may be an as yet unidentified contemporary from the court circles on either side of the English Channel for which Le Sueur worked.

C.A.

RELATED LITERATURE

C. Avery, 'Hubert le Sueur's Portraits of King Charles I in Bronze: At Stourhead, Ickworth and Elsewhere', *National Trust Studies*, 1979, p. 143; reprinted in C. Avery, *Studies in European Sculpture,* vol. I, London 1981, pp. 201–02

C. Avery, 'Hubert Le Sueur, "The Unworthy Praxiteles" of King Charles I', *The Walpole Society*, 1982, pp. 135–209; reprinted in C. Avery, *Studies in European Sculpture,* vol. II, London 1988, pp. 145–235

G. Bresc-Bautier and G. Scherf, eds., *Cast in Bronze, French Sculpture from Renaissance to Revolution* (French edn *Bronzes Français de la Renaissance au Siècle les Lumières*), exh. cat., Musée du Louvre, Paris; Metropolitan Museum of Art, New York; The J.P. Getty Museum, Los Angeles, 2009, pp. 178–79, no. 45

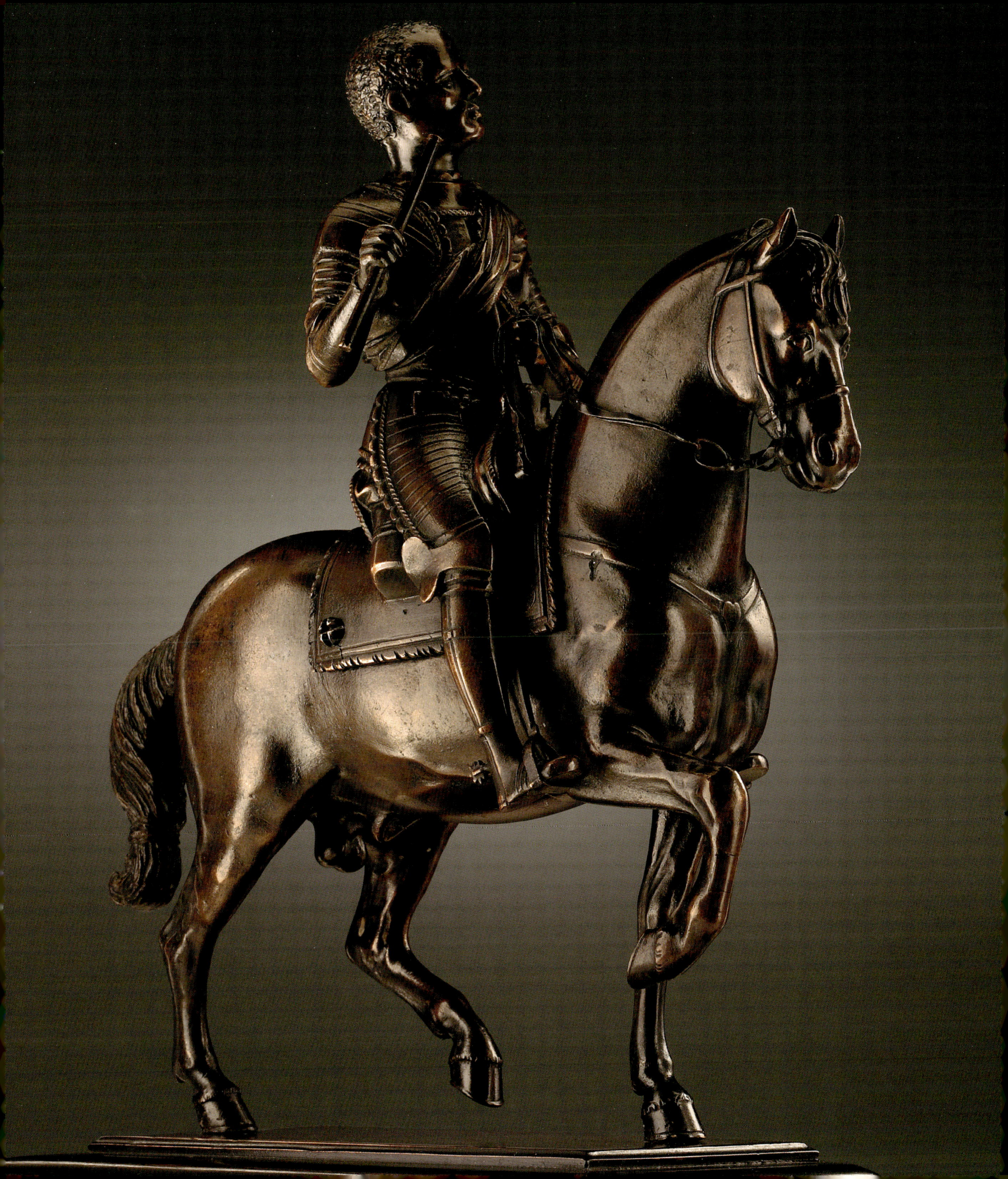

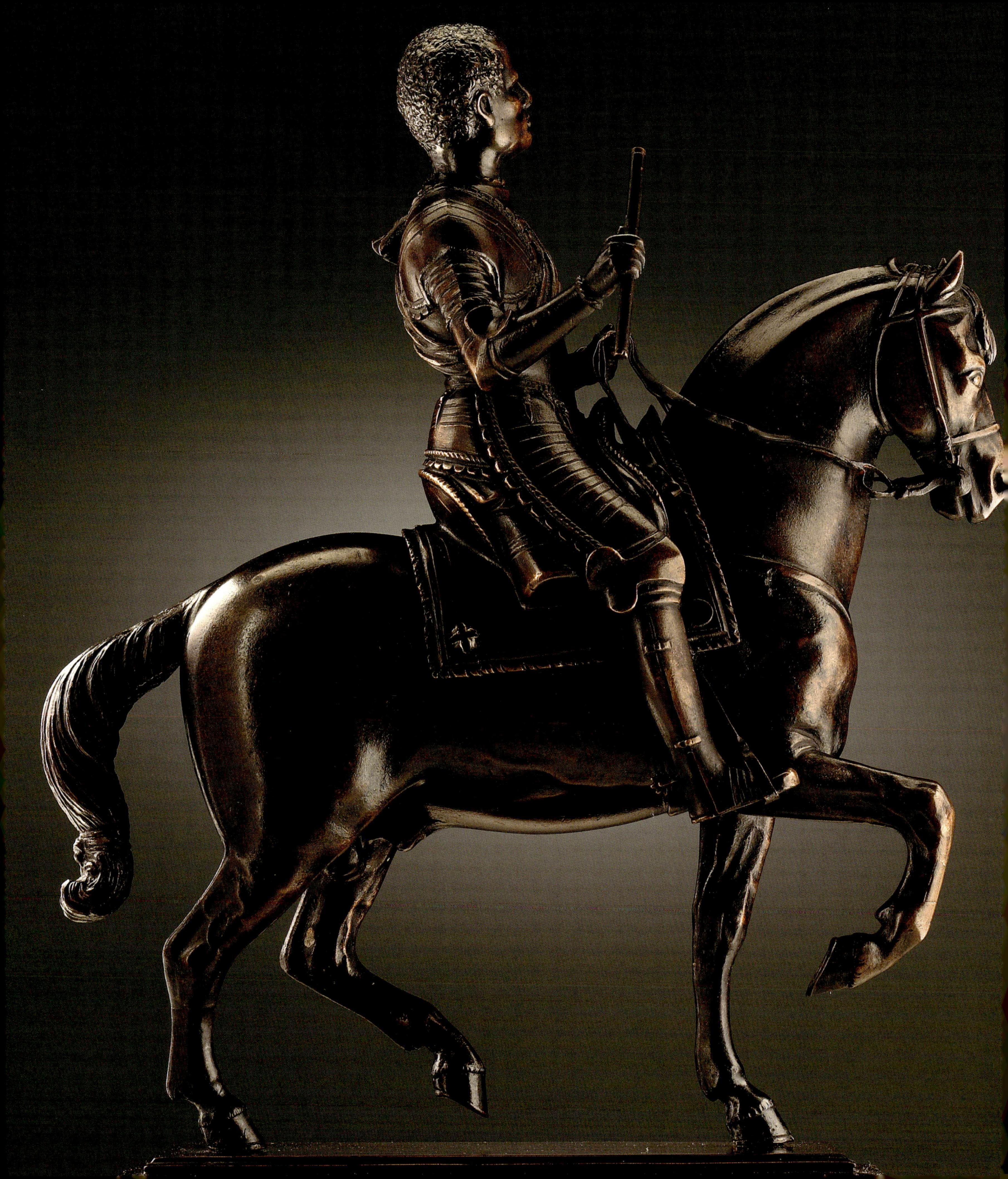

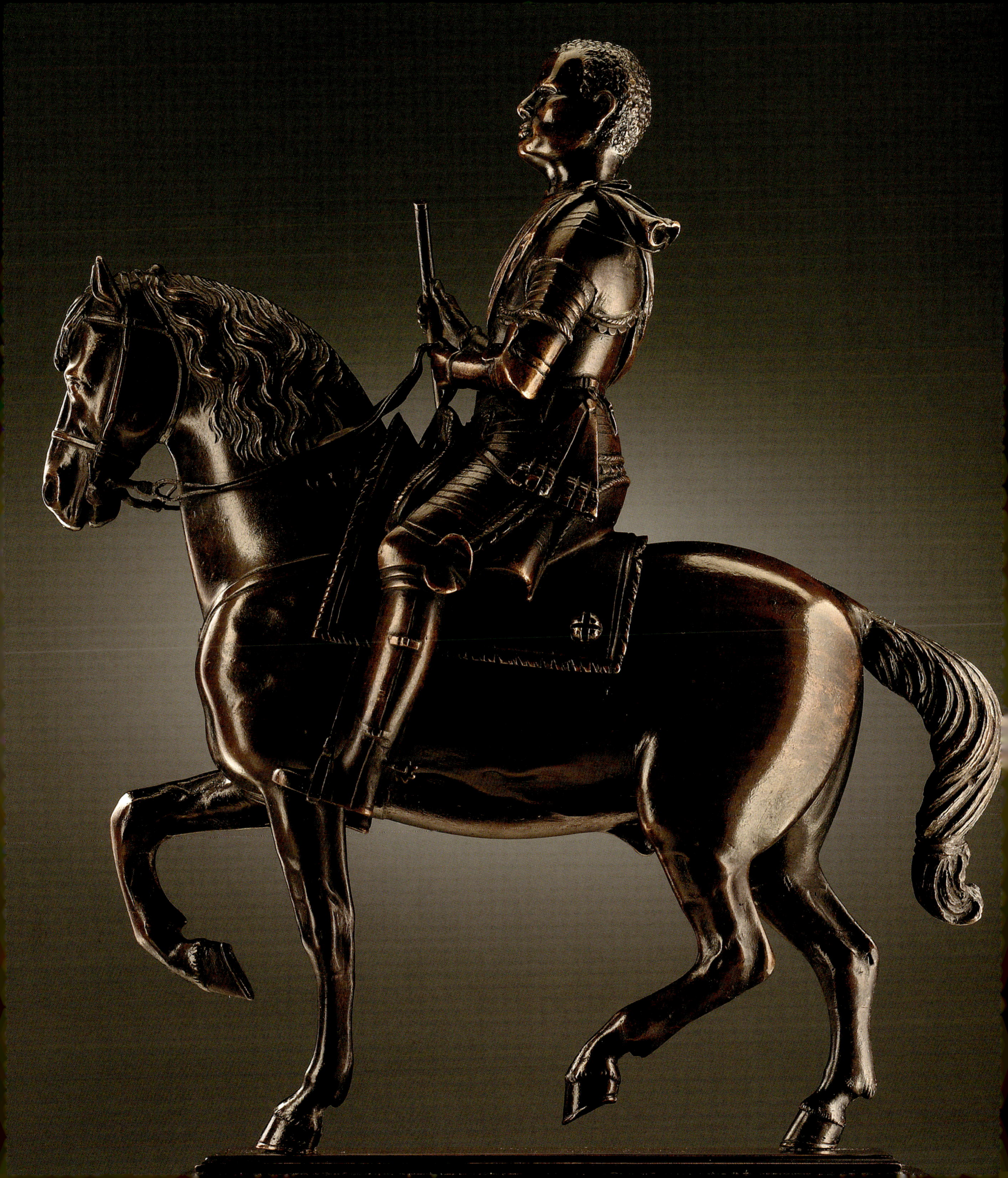

13. GUILLAUME BERTHELOT (*c.* 1583–1648)

(attributed to)

The Borghese Gladiator

Bronze, dark-brown patina with extensive traces of original lacquer

13 ⅛ in. (33 cm)

Guillaume Berthelot, although not widely known to modern scholars and collectors, was, during his lifetime, an important French sculptor, having worked for the kings and queens of France and Cardinal Richelieu. It is recorded that during his youth he was in Rome working on various sculptural projects, including works at Santa Maria Maggiore and Santa Maria in Vallicella. He is credited as the author of the pair of bronzes of Henri IV as Jupiter and Maria de' Medici as Juno which are held by the Walters Art Gallery, Baltimore.

The present bronze is a reduction of the celebrated Borghese *Gladiator,* which, upon its excavation in *c.* 1610, immediately entered Cardinal Borghese's collections. It was then purchased by Napoleon Bonaparte from his brother-in-law Prince Camillo Borghese, in 1807. Since this exchange it has resided in Paris and has always commanded great esteem. Its fame was far reaching and the great French sculptor Hubert Le Sueur is known to have made copies for Charles I of England. In 1638 François Perrier, the great antique enthusiast, published four views of the *Gladiator* – twice as many as he had ever previously dedicated to a statue. It was also counted amongst the primary classical models of which plaster casts were taken by Velázquez for Philip IV of Spain.

Although the antique marble only reached Paris in 1808, the taste for Rome's most famed models reached its zenith in France during the seventeenth century. A number of French bronzes representing the Borghese *Gladiator* are known and most of them seem to originate from this early period. Its size and French origin, along with the Medusa-headed shield, places our bronze close to two models (see related examples) which have been ascribed to Roger Schabol (fl. 1680–after 1714). However, several stylistic attributes of the bronze are closer to the *Diana and Stag* recently ascribed to Berthelot and featured in the *Cast in Bronze, French Sculpture from Renaissance to Revolution* exhibition at the Louvre, the Metropolitan Museum of Art and the J. Paul Getty Museum. The most significant, although subtle, differences in detail are the full delineation of the pupils and the modelling of the individual teeth, which are not found on the later bronzes. It is also noted in the exhibition catalogue that Berthelot's posthumous inventory lists small-scale bronzes of the Borghese *Gladiator.*

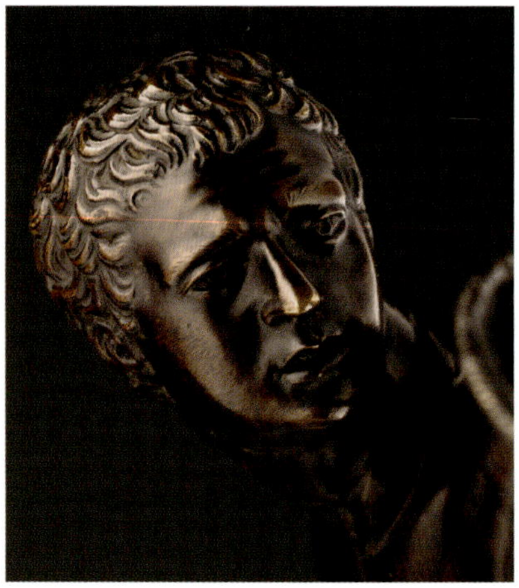

RELATED EXAMPLES

Leithe-Jasper and Wengraf 2005, p. 298, fig. 1
European Sculpture and Works of Art, Sotheby's, London, 8 July 2005, lot 59

RELATED LITERATURE

G. Bresc-Bautier and G. Scherf, eds., *Cast in Bronze, French Sculpture from Renaissance to Revolution* (French edn *Bronzes Français de la Renaissance au Siècle les Lumières*), exh. cat., Musée du Louvre, Paris; Metropolitan Museum of Art, New York; The J.P. Getty Museum, Los Angeles, 2009, pp. 62, 172–75, no. 43

M. Leithe-Jasper and P. Wengraf, *European Bronzes from the Quentin Collection*, exh. cat., Frick Collection, New York, 2004–05, p. 298, fig. 1

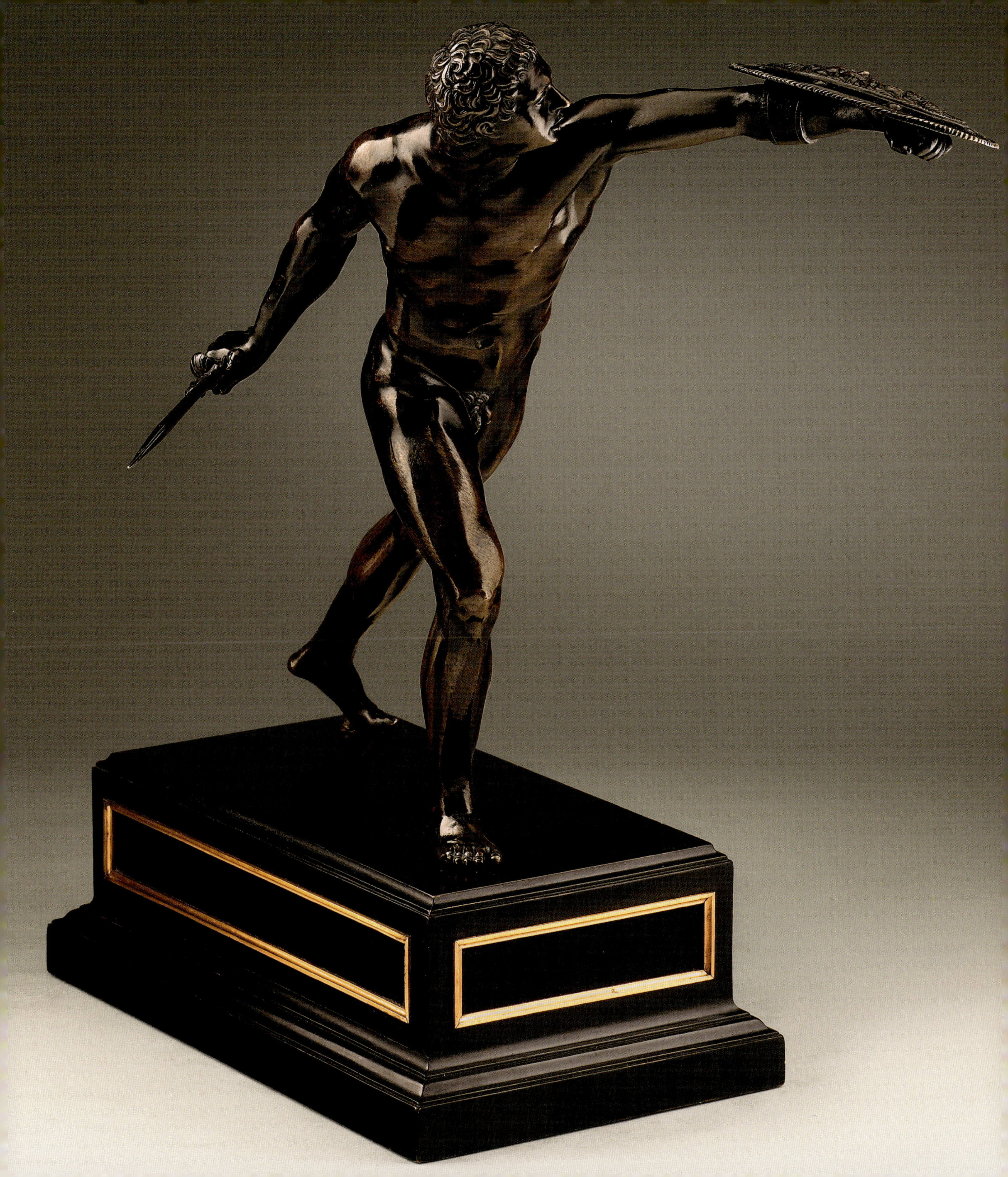

14. GIANFRANCESCO SUSINI (1585–1653)

(attributed to)

Pacing Bull

Bronze, reddish-gold translucent lacquer over olive-brown patina

8 1/8 in. (20.5 cm) high

Gianfrancesco Susini was apprenticed to his uncle Antonio Susini, and then went on to further his training with a trip to Rome to study the ancients in 1624–26. Upon his return, Gianfrancesco inherited the Borgo Pinto workshops in Florence from his uncle. He continued to work in the mould of the great Mannerist sculptor Giambologna, producing his models along with his own inventions.

It is highly likely that the *Pacing Bull* was made to pair with the iconic image of the *Pacing Horse,* which was conceived by Giambologna *c.* 1580. Though the *Pacing Bull* is quite clearly influenced by ancient prototypes, it was successfully modified in the Mannerist fashion. The present beautifully cast and chiselled model originated in Florence during the first half of the seventeeth century. An attribution to Gianfrancesco Susini is highly plausible. The tooling adopted by the sculptor to describe the rocky base on the *Hercules slaying the Centaur* (Quentin Collection, New York) and the base and club of the Farnese *Hercules* (Robert H. Smith Collection, Washington) correspond to that found on the hooves of this present bronze. This typical tooling, depicting a change in texture, and the colour of the patina and its translucent lacquers, would also suggest Susini's hand.

RELATED LITERATURE

C. Avery and A. Radcliffe, eds., *Giambologna (1529–1608): Sculptor to the Medici*, exh. cat., The Arts Council, London, and Kunsthistorisches Museum, Vienna, 1978, repr. p. 192, no. 178

M. Leithe-Jasper and P. Wengraf, *European Bronzes from the Quentin Collection*, exh. cat., Frick Collection, New York, 2004–05, pp. 166–75, no. 15

A. Radcliffe, *The Robert H. Smith Collection of Bronzes 1500–1650*, London 1994, pp. 78–81, no. 14

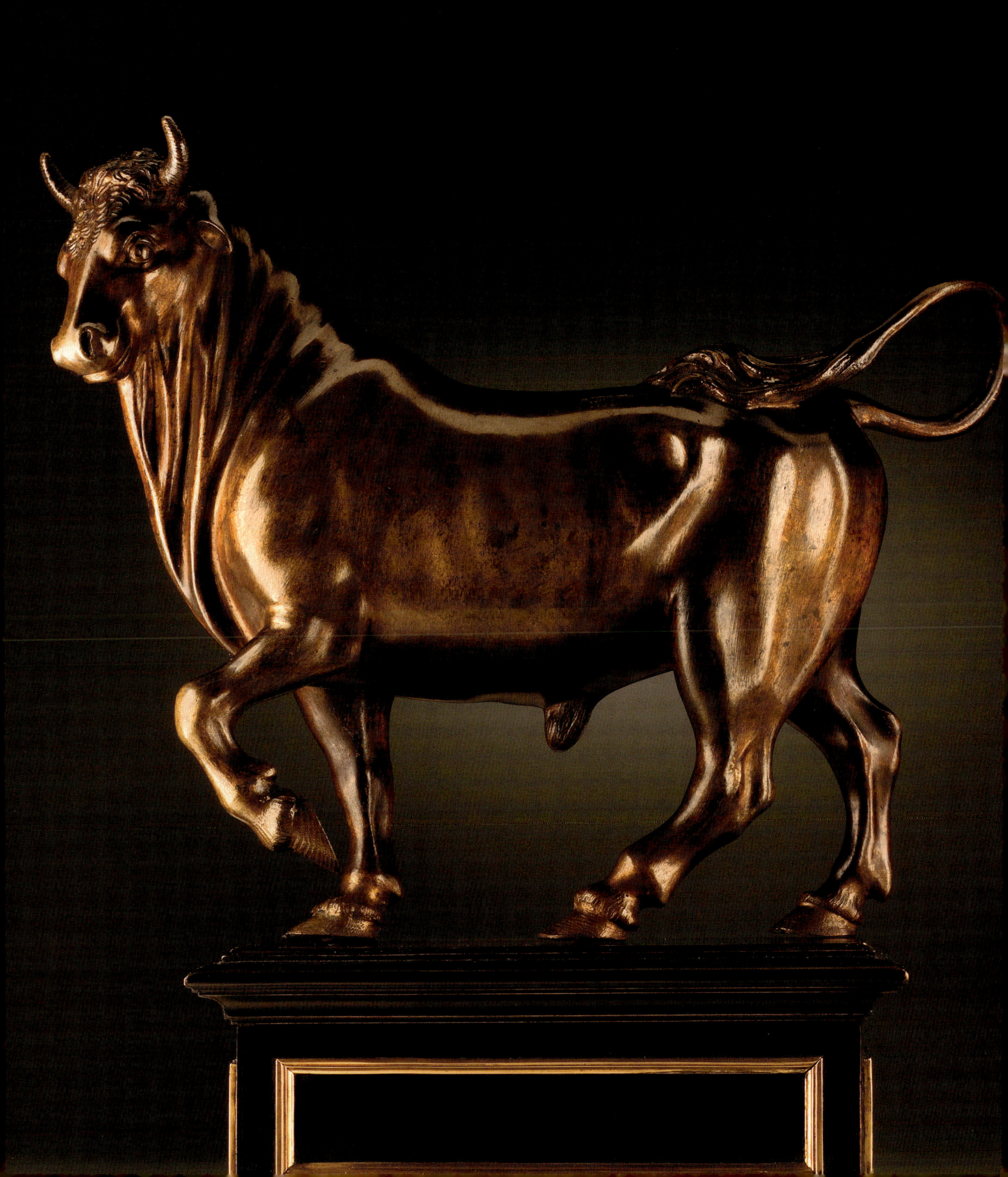

15. ROMAN, 17th century

The Pietà (after MICHELANGELO)

Bronze, rich brown patina

14 ¾ in. (37.5 cm) high

Michelangelo's *Pietà*, along with his figure of *David*, is the most important and highly esteemed piece of sculpture from the Renaissance. The composition of the mother of Christ lamenting the death of her son as he lies lifeless in her arms exudes the highest sense of pathos to be found in any rendition of the subject. The original marble, now in St Peter's, Rome, was carved by Michelangelo in his early to mid twenties upon a commission from the French Cardinal Jean Villiers de La Grolais for his tomb. It is widely considered that this masterpiece was the beginning of Michelangelo's maturity as a sculptor. The effect of many different textures portrayed through one piece of marble has not been surpassed by any other artist since, and is conveyed through the proximity of different surfaces and perceived weights, calculated with enormous skill. Certain details within the overall scheme emphasize the feeling of loss, already conveyed in the fragile lifelessness and weight of Christ's body being clutched by the motherly strength, albeit in grief, of the Madonna. These include the damp loincloth of Christ against his supremely polished skin, and these contrasted against the voluminous, almost mountainous-like sculpting of his mother's drapery and solemn gaze.

At present it is not possible to ascribe an author to this beautiful Baroque bronze reduction of the *Pietà,* but it is almost certain that it was cast in Rome in the early to mid seventeenth century, probably within the Bernini–Algardi circle. There is an early seventeenth-century life-size cast of Michelangelo's work by Gregorio de' Rossi in the church of Sant'Andrea della Valle, Rome.

RELATED LITERATURE

C. Acidini Luchinat, *Michelangelo Scultore*, Milan 2006, pp. 58–67, repr. pp. 58–67

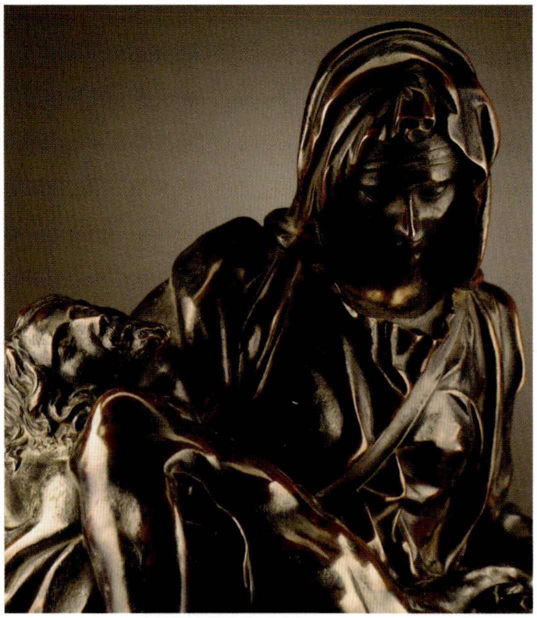

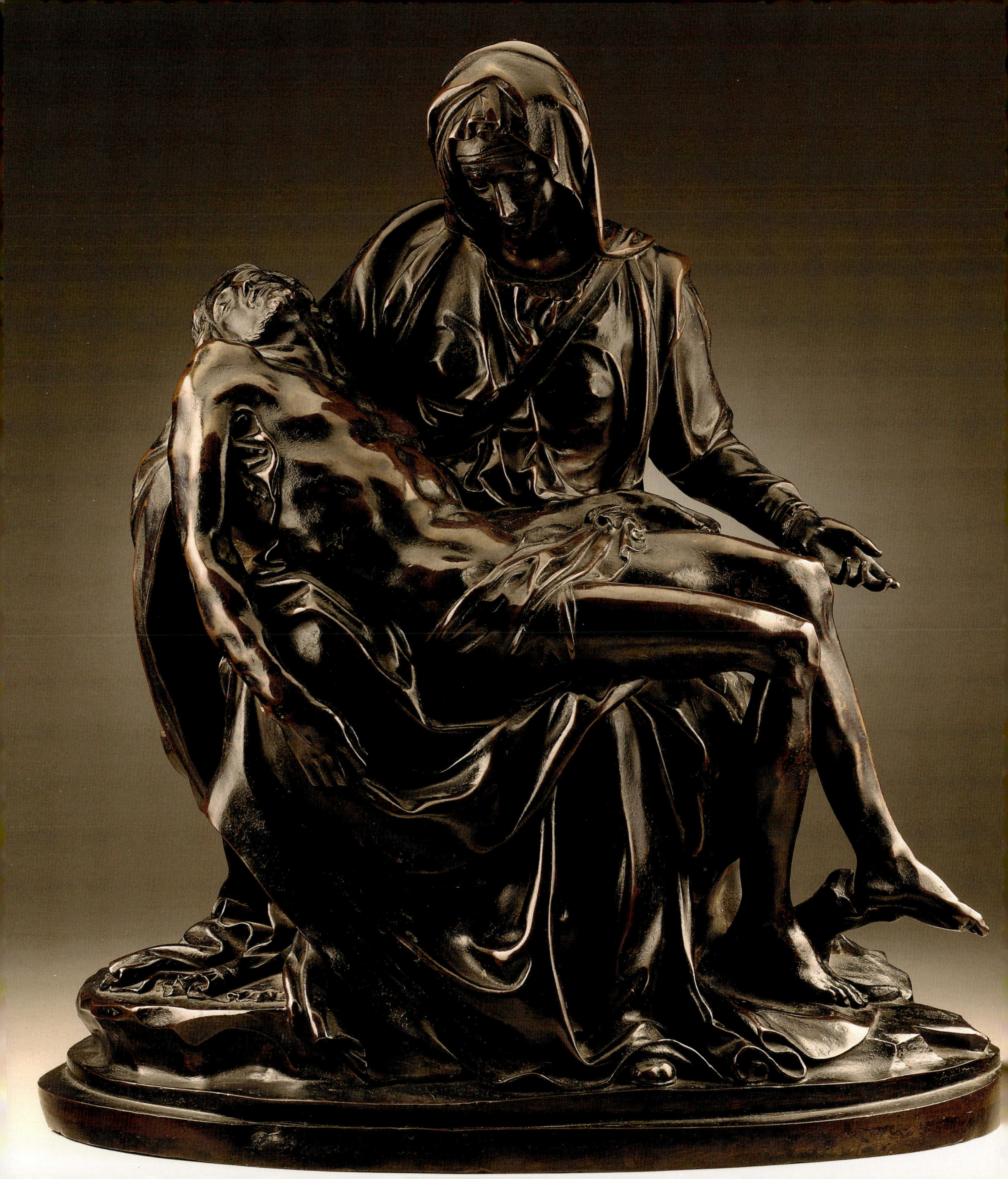

16. FRANÇOIS ĐUQUESNOY (1597–1643)

(attributed to)

Cupid carving his Bow

Bronze on integrally cast rectangular base, on wood socle, olive-brown patina beneath traces of translucent golden lacquer

10 ¾ in (27. 3 cm) high

This statuette is a reduction of superb quality of a 76 cm-high marble statue by François Duquesnoy, carved in Italy about 1625 and now in the Staatliche Museum, Berlin, inv. no. 540.

According to Joachim von Sandrart, painter, biographer and personal friend of the sculptor, Duquesnoy undertook this ambitiously undercut composition in order to disprove accusations by Italian rivals that he was not up to carving in marble: despite this demonstration they continued to slander him and the statue remained in his hands until, in 1629, Sandrart himself negotiated its sale to the opulent Dutch art collector Lucas van Uffel, who was living in Venice at that time. Van Uffel brought the marble statue back to Holland, and after his death in 1637 it was purchased by the city of Amsterdam and presented to Princess Amalia of Orange. She took it to The Hague, and after her death it entered in 1689 the collection of King Frederick of Prussia, who kept it in his Kunstkammer (inventory of 1694, f. 177, no. 6).

The particular theme was probably inspired by a description of a statue by Lysippus of Eros stringing his bow. It has recently been demonstrated that the composition derived from

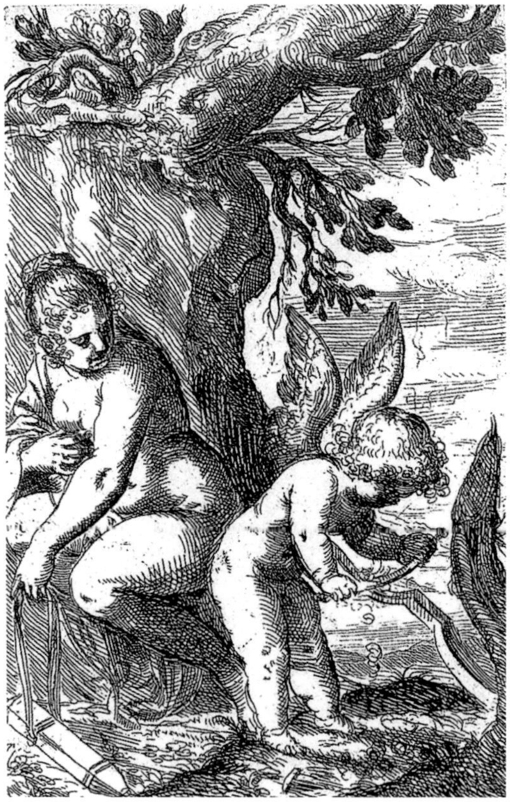

Venus regarding Amor, who is cutting a bow, from Odoardo Fialetti's *Scherzi d'Amore,* Venice 1617

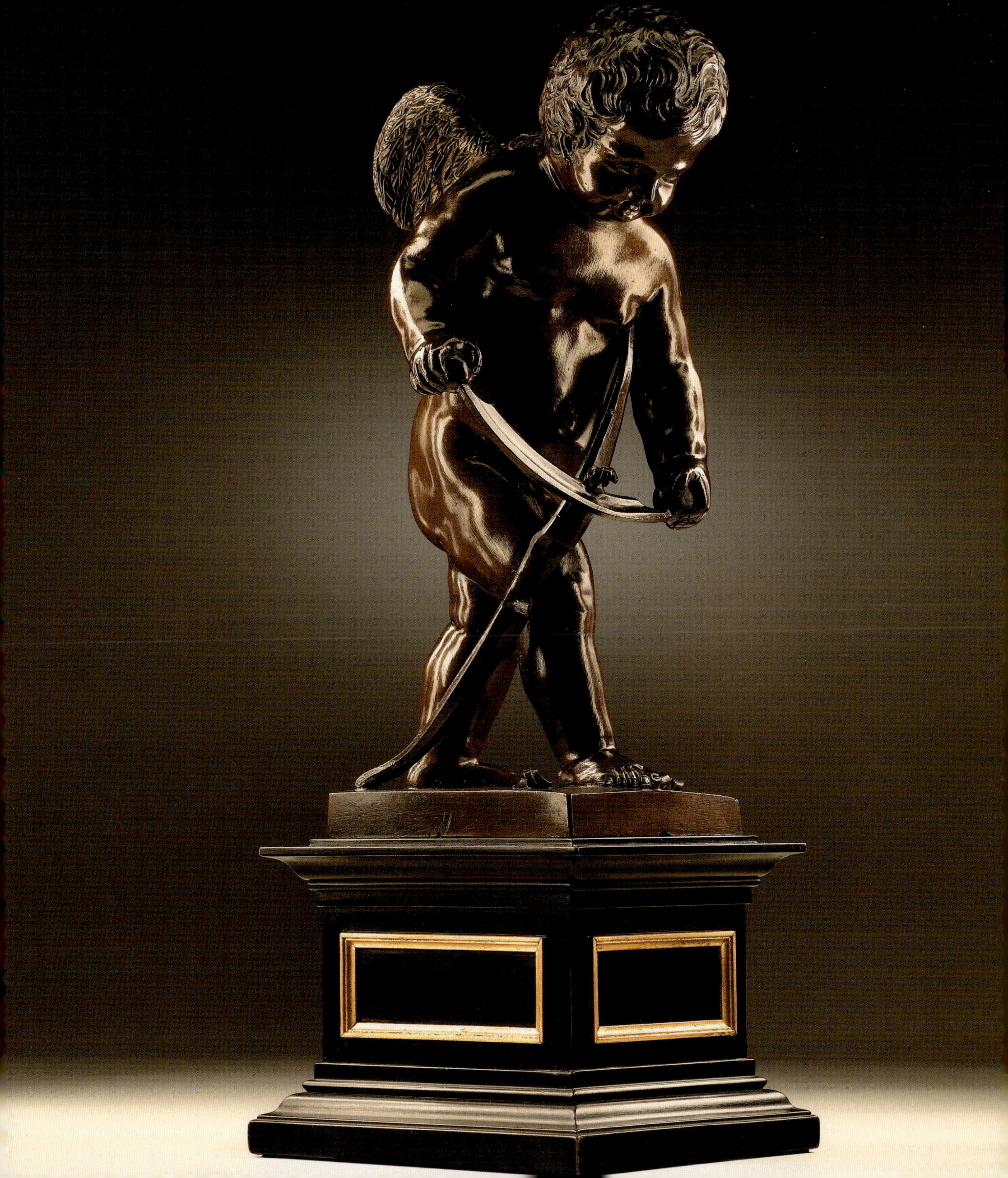

a Venetian etching of 1617 showing Cupid cutting his new bow to replace one confiscated (and broken) by his mother Venus (illus.; see Lingo 2007, p. 61, fig. 48). Highly appreciated by contemporaries, the statue was copied in Germany as early as the second half of the seventeenth century. The full-size model appears on the top of a cabinet in the background of the painting known as *'The Van Goyen Family'* by Jan Steen, now in the Nelson Atkins Museum of Art, Kansas City.

Bellori records small-scale models of putti which were made to be reproduced in copper and silver, as well as a bronze *Mercury and Cupid* made for Vincenzo Giustiniani, and a figure of *Apollo;* the finest versions of the *Mercury* and the *Apollo,* generally accepted as being by Duquesnoy himself, are in the Liechtenstein Collection (Krahn 1995, pp. 502–05, nos. 181–82).

C.A.

LITERATURE

A. Bacchi, ed., *Scultura del '600 a Roma,* Milan 1996, pp. 796–99, pl. 323

E. Borea and C. Gasparri, *L'idea del Bello. Viaggio a Roma nel Seicento con Giovan Pietro Bellori,* exh. cat., Palazzo delle Esposizioni, Rome 2000, p. 199, no. 1 (entry by V. Krahn)

M.Boudon-Machuel, *François du Quesnoy, 1597–1643,* Paris 2005, p. 79, fig. 77; p. 273, cat. OE. 62, OE. 62 dér. 5

V. Krahn, ed., *Von Allen Seiten Schön, Bronzen der Renaissance und des Barock,* exh. cat., Staatliche Museen zu Berlin Preussischer Kulturbesitz, Berlin 1995

E. Lingo, *François Duquesnoy and The Greek Ideal,* New Haven and London 2007, pp. 57–63, figs. 45–48

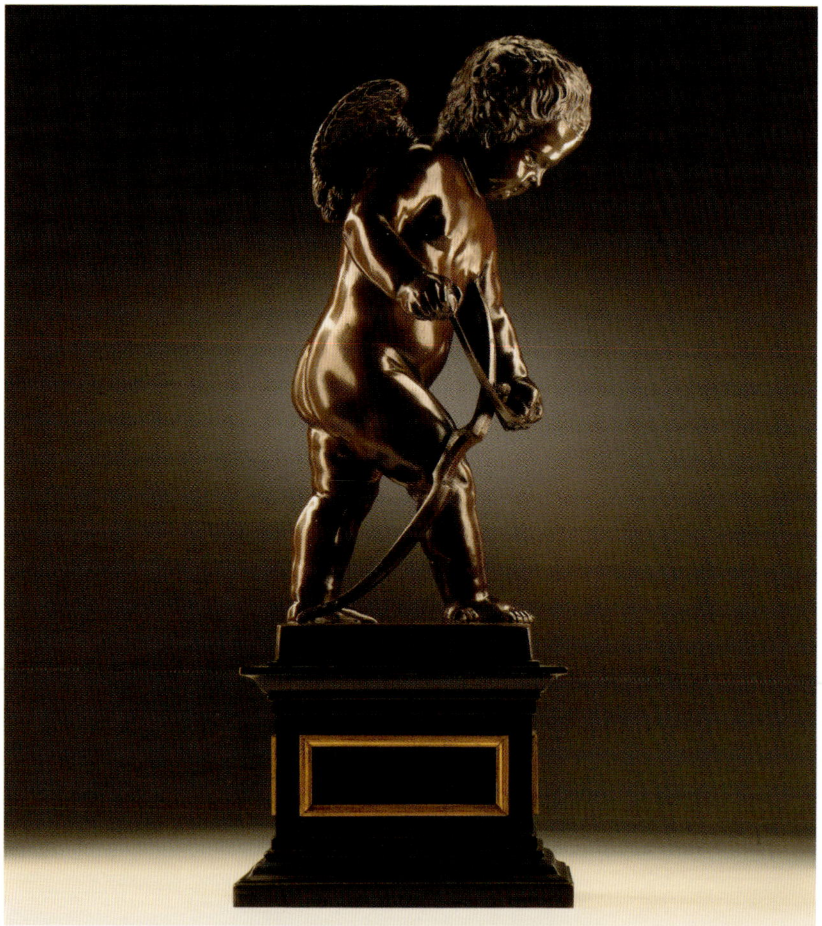

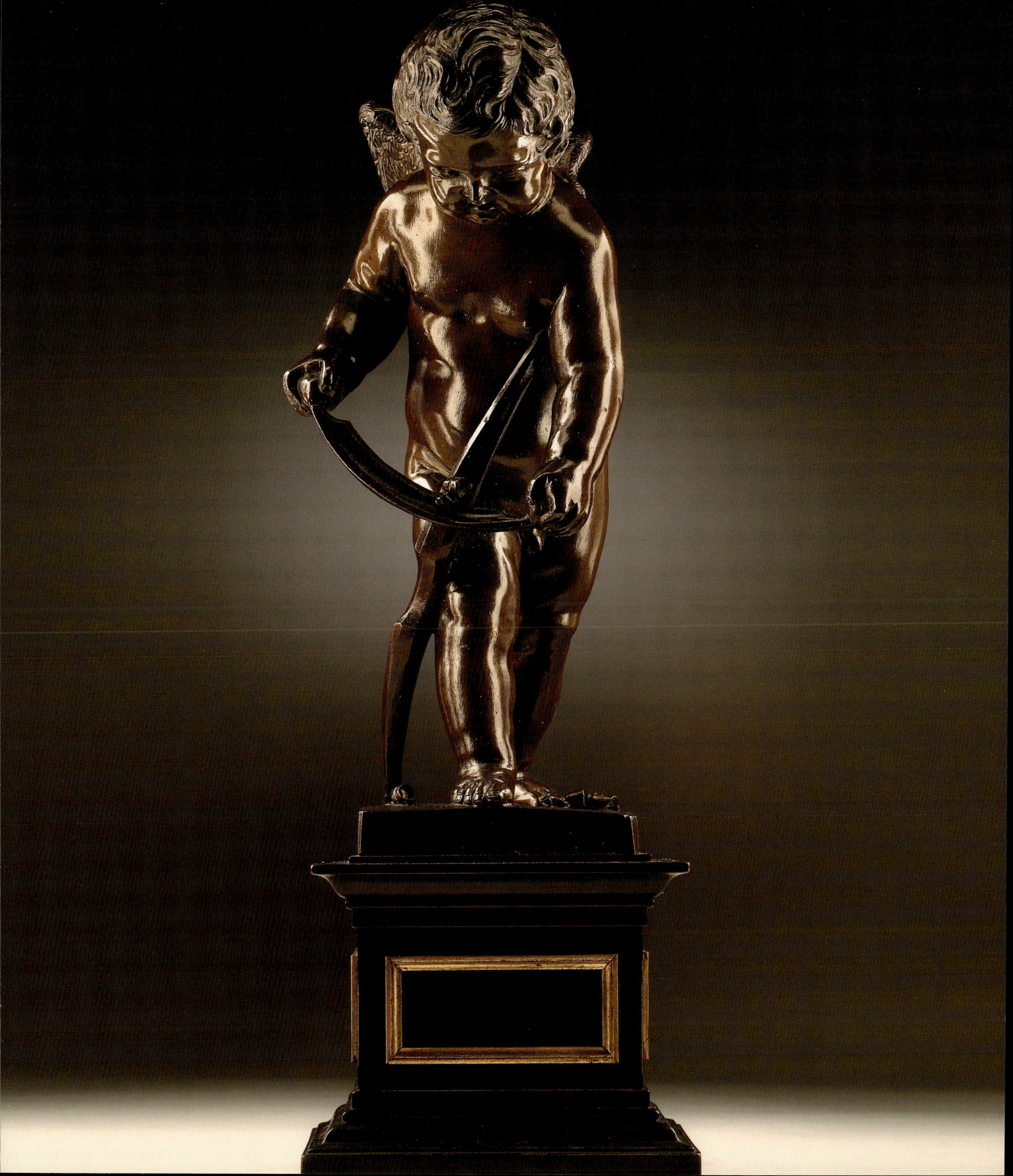

17. GIUSEPPE ANTONIO TORRICELLI (1662–1719)

Christ as the Man of Sorrows

Pietra dura, black marble

12 in. (30 cm) high, 9 ½ in. (24 cm) wide

Giuseppe Antonio Torricelli was charged with the execution of works in *pietra dura* for the Medici in their Grand Ducal workshops in Florence, which were under the directorship of Giovanni Battista Foggini at the time. They were internationally renowned from the sixteenth and eighteenth centuries for producing the highest-quality *pietra dura* objects, such as table tops, caskets, reliquaries, inlaid landscapes and floral designs. High-relief figures of *pietra dura*, like the present example, became particularly fashionable at the end of the seventeenth and beginning of the eighteenth centuries, and Torricelli was the most famous exponent of the medium. He produced a virtuoso bust of Vittoria della Rovere in 1697, which is now in the Museo degli Argenti, Florence. This documented bust, along with other known works, allows us to attribute the present remarkable plaque to this extraordinary master.

The selection for the present relief of the highest-quality stones available, which include a very finely veined *giallo antico*, the purest of *rosso antico*, and basanite (a rare stone from antiquity), is indicative of the gem-like quality of materials associated with the Grand Ducal workshops. Torricelli's productions at this time, including the present plaque, were one of the high points in the history of decorative arts on this intimate scale.

RELATED LITERATURE

Italian Paintings and Sculpture of the 17th & 18th Centuries, Tenth Summer Exhibition, exh. cat., Heim Gallery, London, 1976, no. 35

A. Giusti, *L'arte delle pietre dure: Da Firenze all'Europa*, Florence 2005, p. 102, no. 83

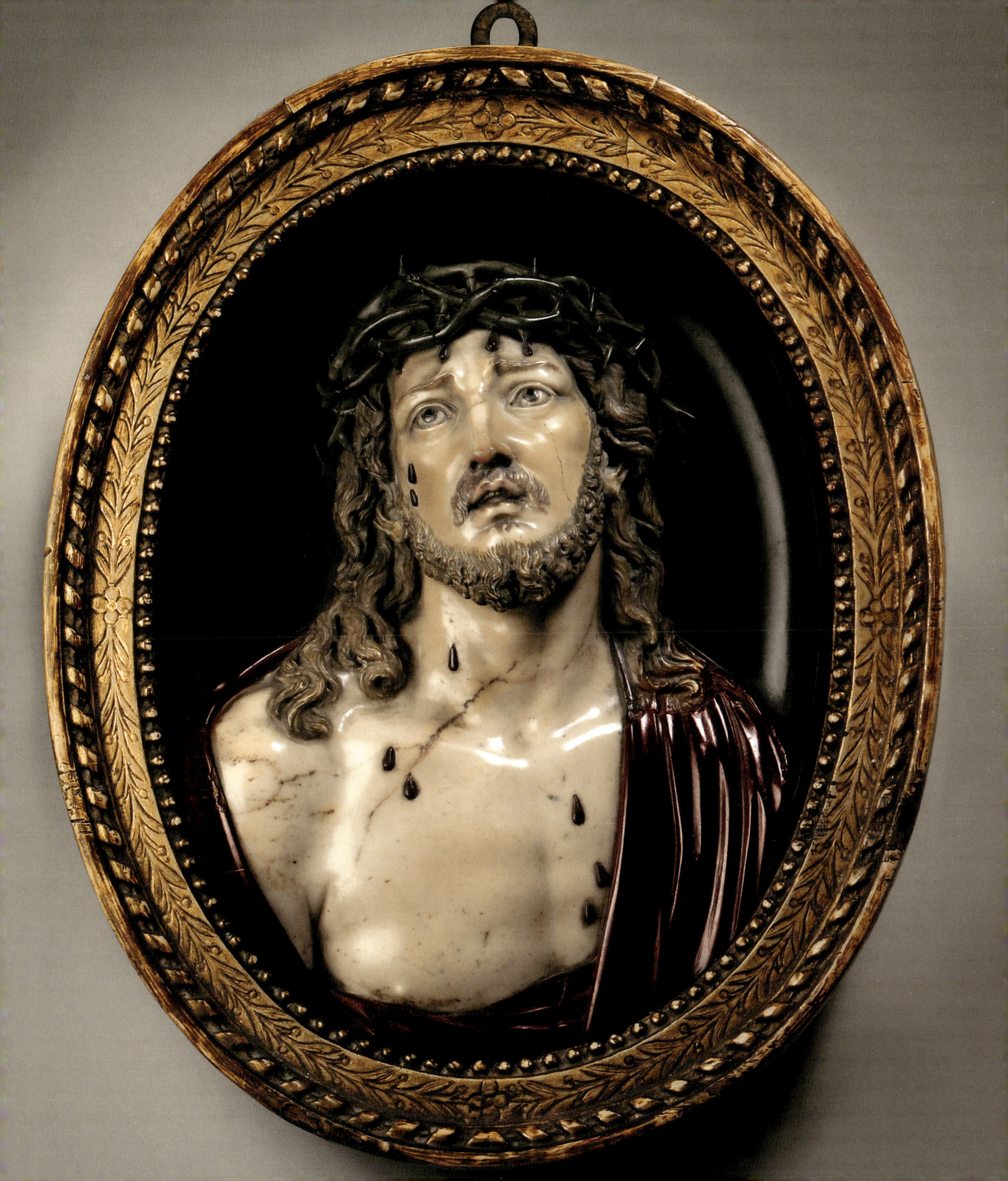

18. FRANÇOIS GIRARDON (1628–1715)

(attributed to)

c. 1690–1700

The Rape of Proserpina

Bronze, brown patina with traces of red lacquer

41 3/8 in. (105 cm) high

François Girardon was the greatest French sculptor of his day and was instrumental in forming the classical style of academic sculpture fashionable in the reign of the Sun King, Louis XIV, and especially of those works connected with Versailles. In 1657 he was accepted into the Académie Royale, where his *morceau de réception* was a marble oval profile medallion of *The Virgin of Sorrows*. His importance as France's leading sculptor is evident in two highly prestigious commissions – one for the funerary monument to Cardinal de Richelieu, in the Chapel of the Sorbonne, Paris, the other for the monumental bronze equestrian statue of the king in Roman armour, made for the Place de Vendôme, sadly destroyed during the Revolution.

The bronze presented here is a contemporary cast of one of Girardon's most spectacular and sophisticated compositions. Quite clearly inspired by Giambologna's masterpiece *The Rape of the Sabine* in the Loggia dei Lanzi, Florence, this *tour de force* by Girardon was possibly the most important piece of sculpture at Versailles. The original marble, which was begun in 1677 and finally signed and dated in 1699, depicts the moment in ancient mythology when Pluto abducts Proserpina and carries her off to the underworld to become his wife.

There are four known contemporary casts of this bronze – the example from the French royal collection made for Louis XIV in 1692; an example that belonged to Édouard Colbert de Villacerf; and two examples owned by the artist and mentioned in his inventory of 1715.

We know from documentation that the example from the French royal collection is now held by the Versailles Museum, and it has been argued that the two which were in Girardon's own collection are those now held by the Château des Rohan, Strasbourg, and the Heckscher Museum, Huntington, California. The present bronze is closest to that in Strasbourg, especially in the modelling of the rockwork base. The model shown in Nicolas Chevalier's etching (illus.) has a base similar to both the Strasbourg and the present bronze. The obvious difference between the present bronze and the four exhibited in the recent *Cast in Bronze* exhibition is that, while the others are section cast, ours is cast in one piece. It is generally accepted that primary examples are cast in one and that later casts tend to be made sectionally, even when produced at an early date. It is therefore plausible that the present example is the first large-scale bronze reduction of the marble and possibly that which was exhibited at the Académie in 1699 and 1704.

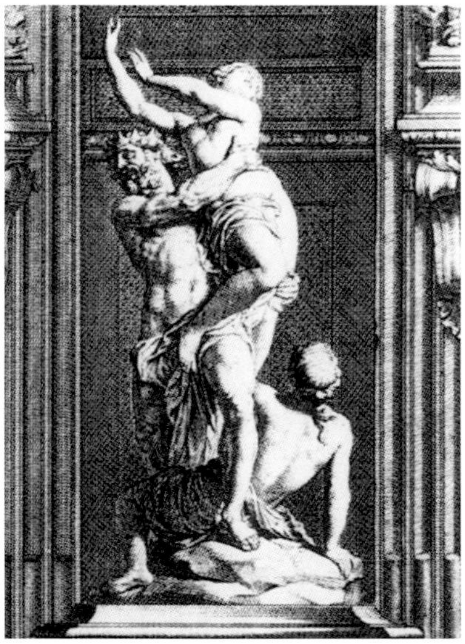

Nicolas Chevalier, *Girardon's Collection*, detail, *c.* 1710

COMPARATIVE LITERATURE

G. Bresc-Bautier and G. Scherf, eds., *Cast in Bronze, French Sculpture from Renaissance to Revolution* (French edn *Bronzes Français de la Renaissance au Siècle les Lumières*), exh. cat., Musée du Louvre, Paris, Metropolitan Museum of Art, New York and The J.P. Getty Museum, Los Angeles, 2009, no. 68

Europäische Barockplastik am Niederrhein: Grupello und seine Zeit, exh. cat., Dusseldorf, Kunstmuseum, 1971, pp. 368–69, no. 334, pl. 215

F. Souchal, 'La Collection du Sculpteur Girardon d'après son Inventaire après décès', *Gazette des Beaux Arts*, LXXXII, 1973, pp. 1–112

F. Souchal, *French Sculptors of the 17th and 18th Centuries: The Reign of Louis XIV*, Oxford 1981–93, vol. II, pp. 41–43, no. 42, and supplementary vol., London 1993, pp. 102–04, no. 42

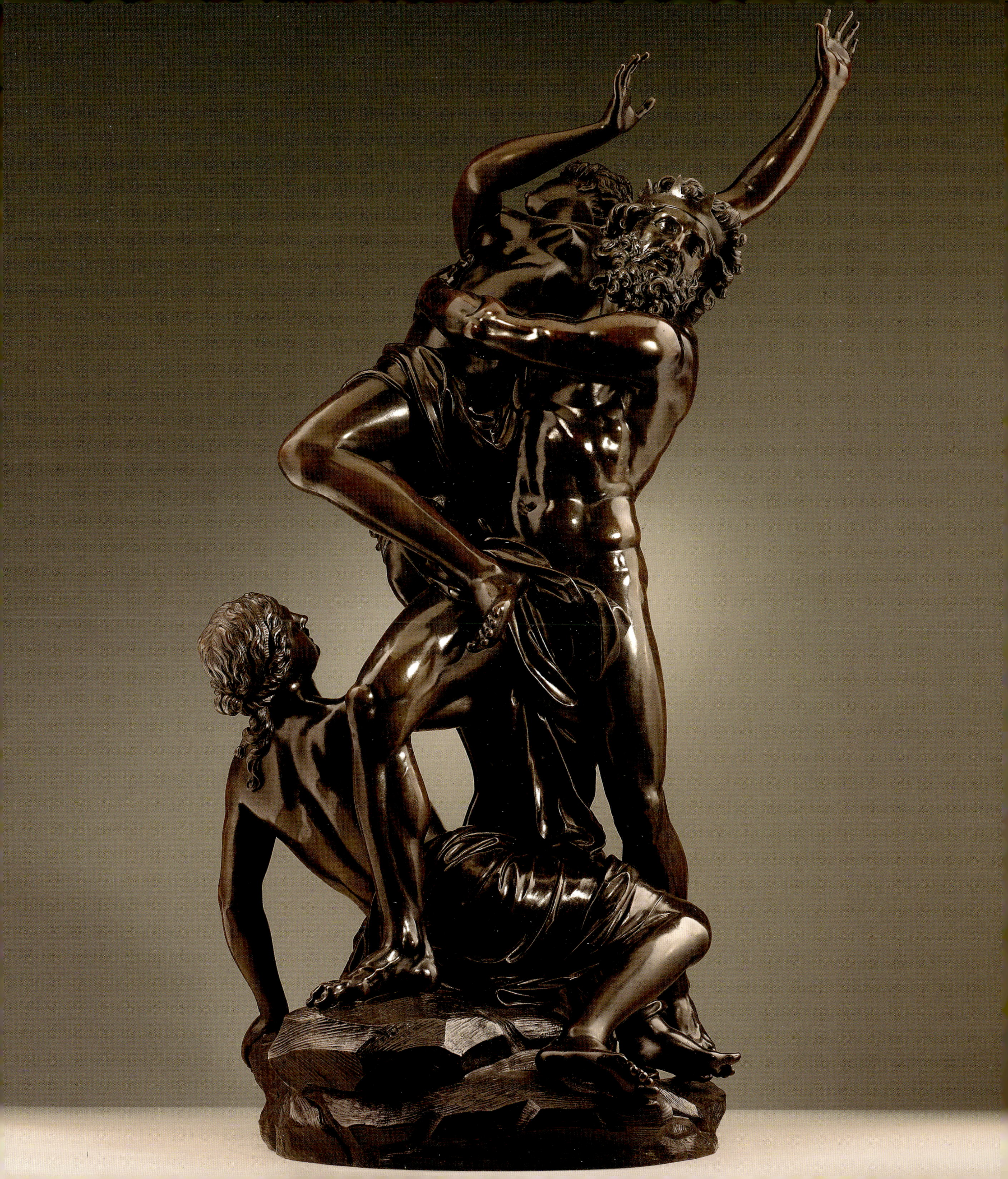

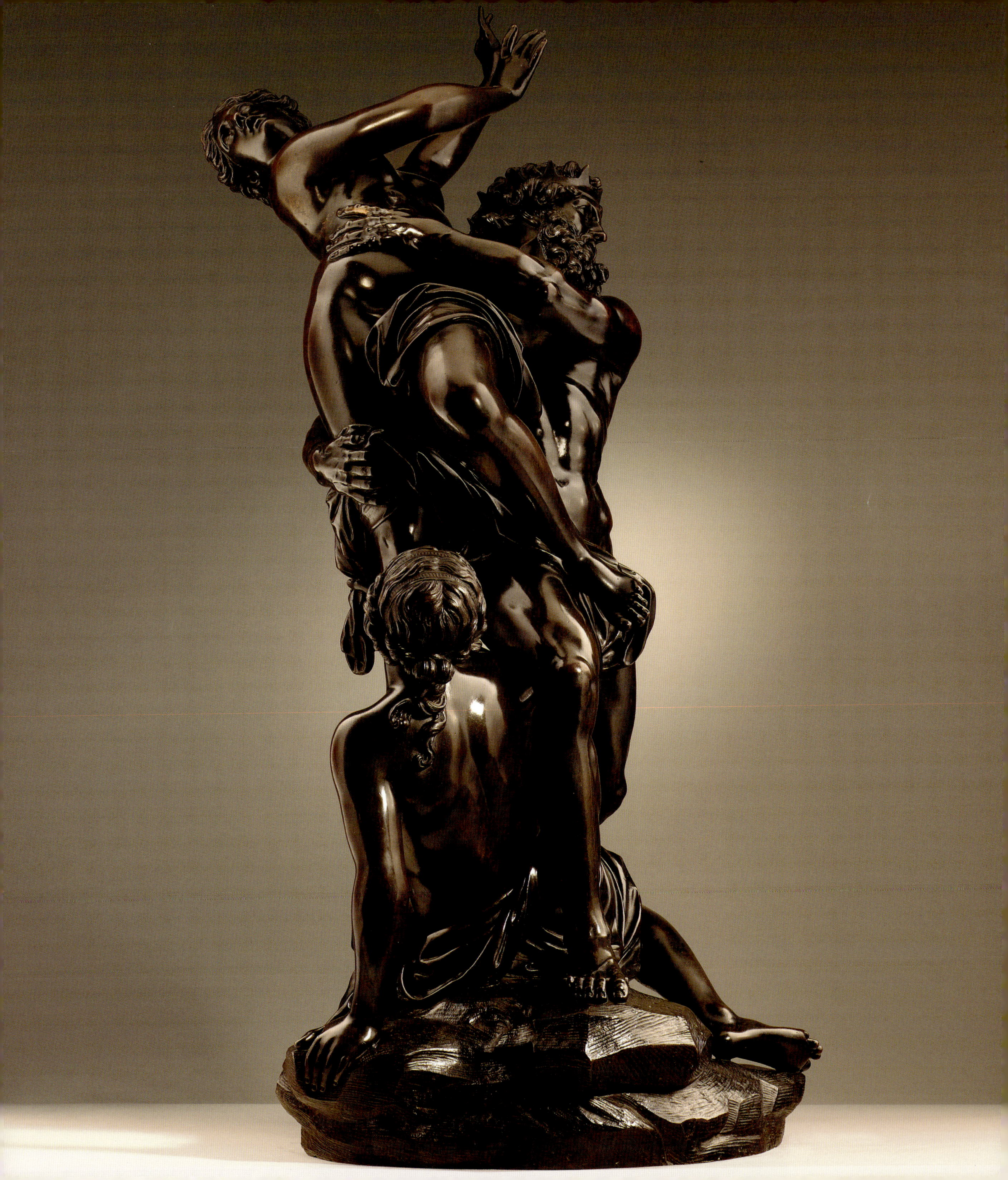

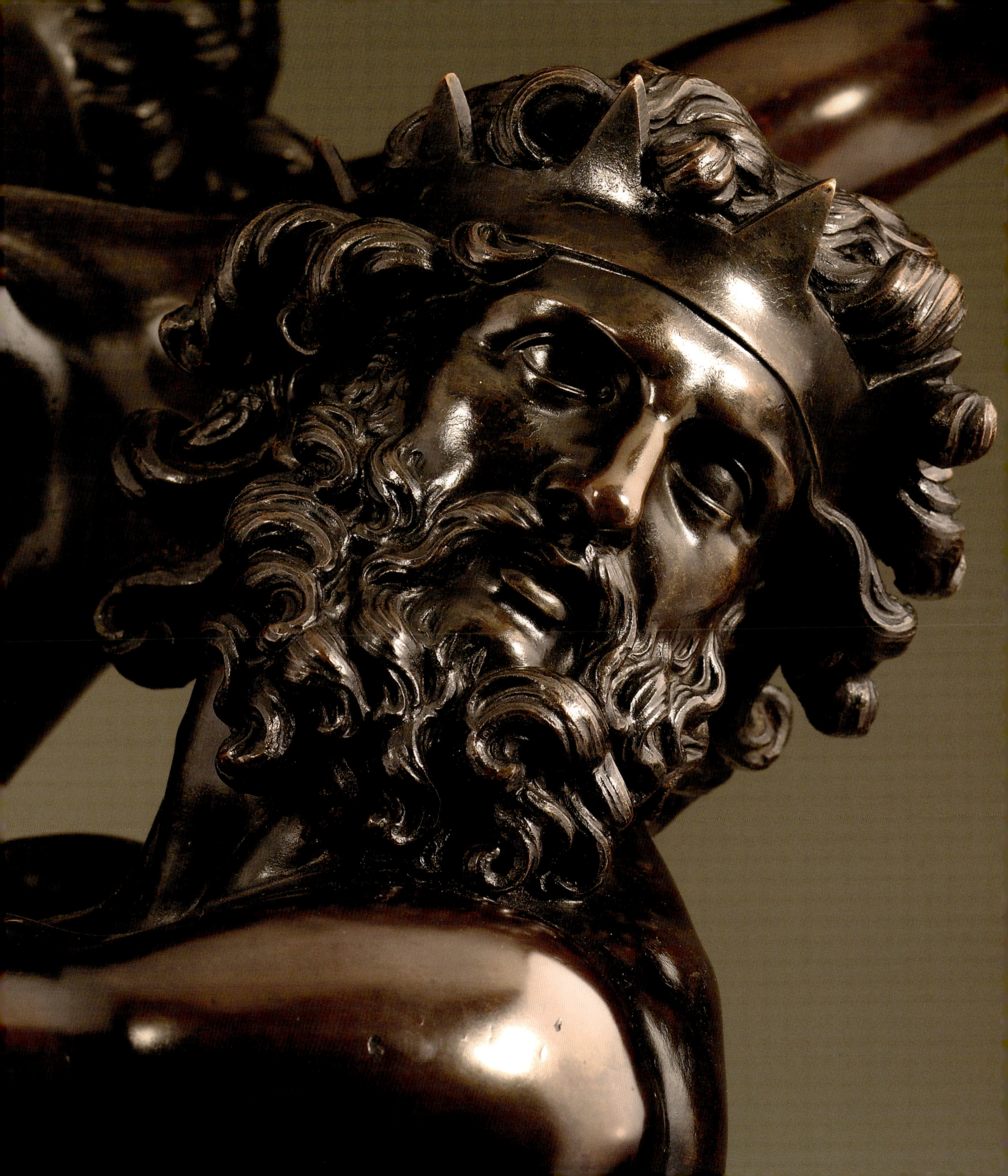

19. FRANÇOIS GIRARDON (1628–1715)

(Workshop of)

Marsyas

Bronze, greenish-brown patina with black lacquer

23 5/8 in. (60 cm) high

The great sculptor François Girardon was also an incredibly enthusiastic collector in his own right, and his extensive collection of sculpture was recorded in an album of engravings published by Nicolas Chevalier after Charpentier's and Oppenord's drawings entitled *La Galerie de Girardon sculpteur ordinaire du Roy.*

The exhibition bronze is a reduction of an ancient model depicting Marsyas about to be flayed, having lost his musical competition against Apollo. There are a small number of fragmentary antique examples in marble, most notably the one bought by the Medici from the della Valle collection, Rome. The Medici example was in Rome at the time of Girardon's early visit to the city, *c.* 1647–50, and is probably the inspiration behind his terracotta of *Marsyas*, reproduced in the celebrated engraving of his gallery (plate III), where it can be seen placed in the right-hand niche (illus.). This allows us to connect the model directly to Girardon, and, as this subject remains rarely depicted, the present bronze was probably cast in his workshop.

RELATED EXAMPLE

John R. Gaines Collection, Christie's, New York, 2 June 1993, lot 206; now in the Abbott Guggenheim Collection, Warwick, New York

RELATED LITERATURE

F. Haskell and N. Penny, *Taste and the Antique*, New Haven and London 1981, p. 262, no. 59, fig. 136

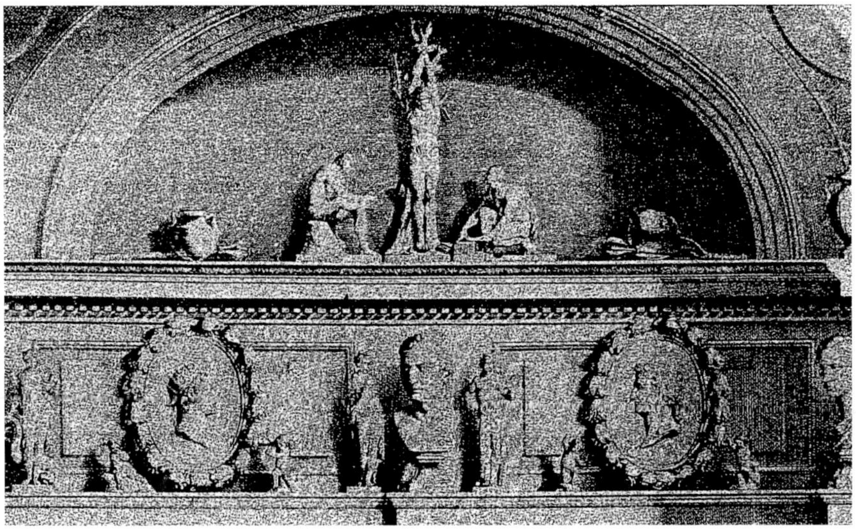

Nicolas Chevalier after Charpentier and Oppenord, *La Galerie de Girardon sculpteur ordinaire du Roy*, detail of Plate III

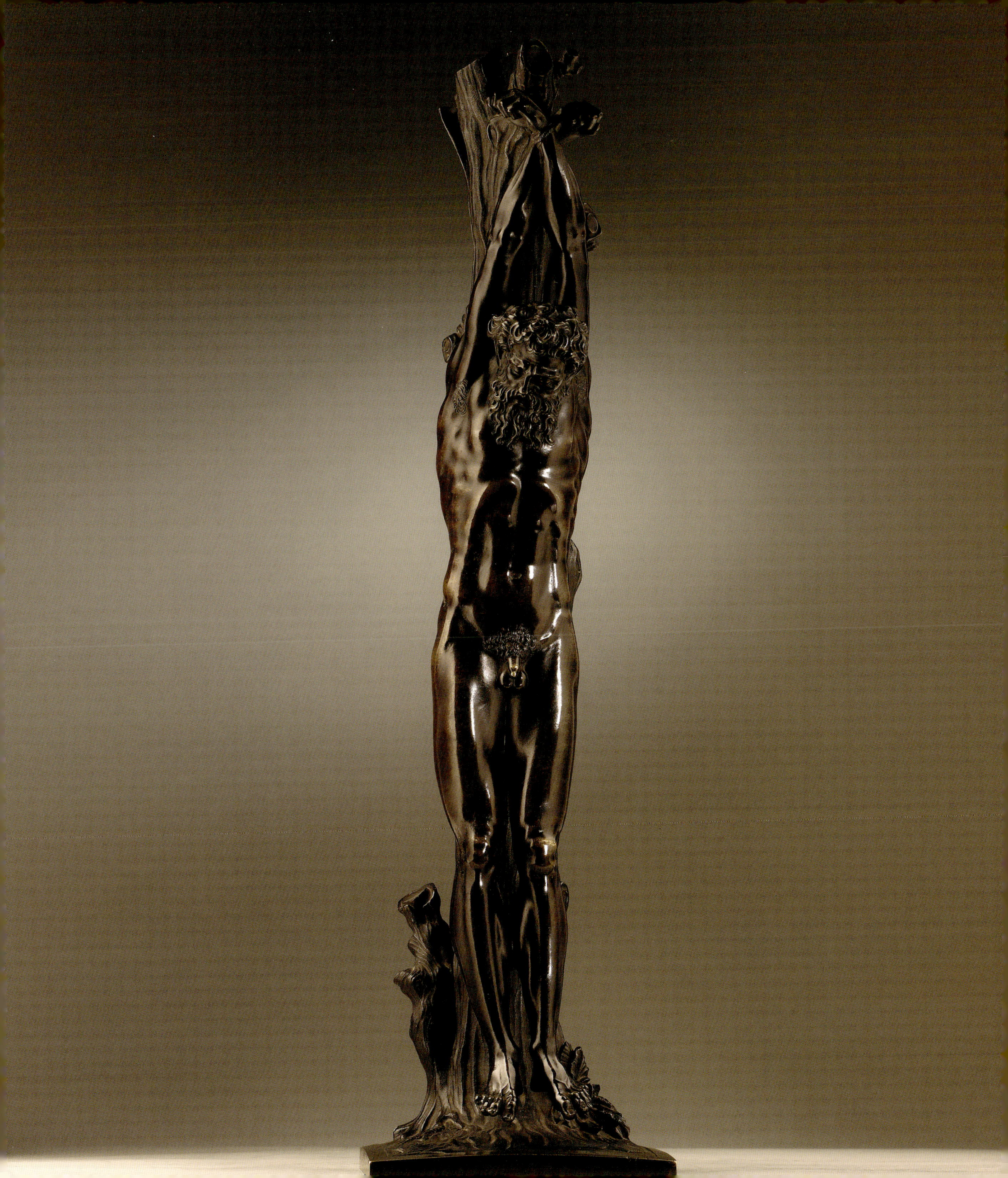

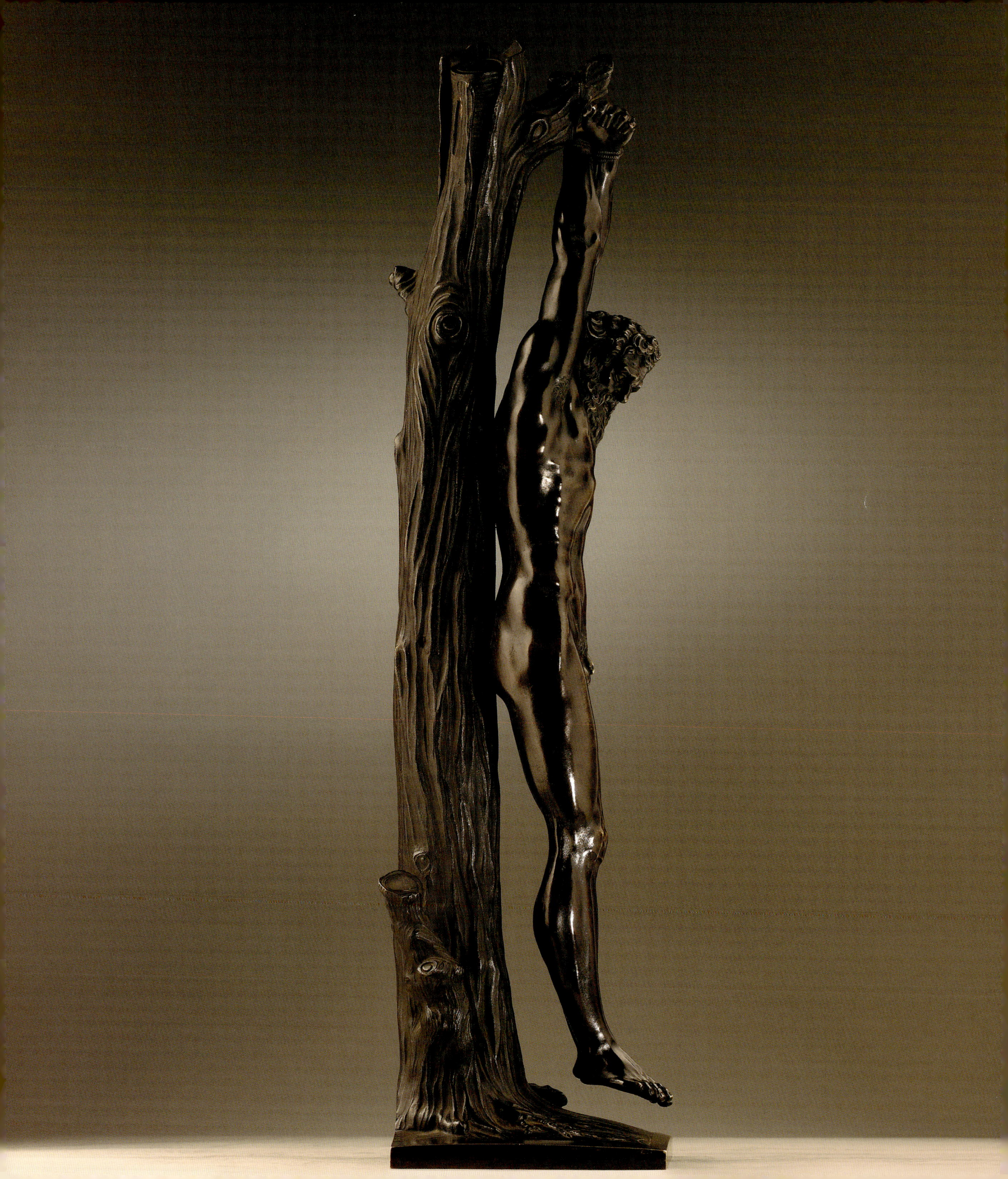

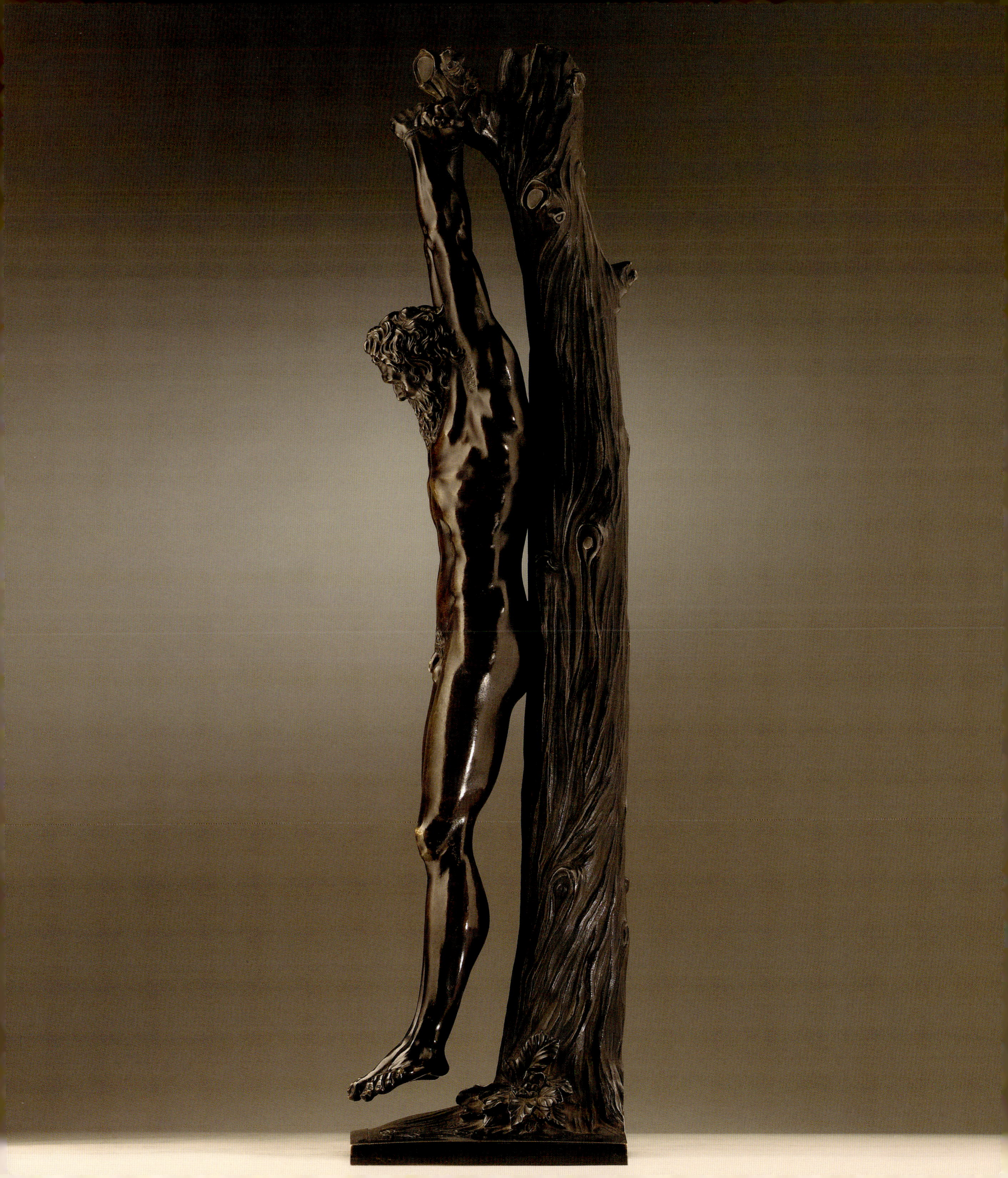

20. JEAN RAON (1630–1707)

(Circle of)

A Bust of a Young Faun wearing a Pine Wreath and a Goatskin

White marble

28 ½ in. (72.5 cm)

PROVENANCE: Feray collection, Hôtel Tannevot, Paris

This spirited French bust, which depicts a mischievous faun, is based on ancient prototypes, of which the most famous is the Albani example in Rome. Our bust was sculpted in France during the reign of Louis XIV, when the *gôut Italien* was at the height of fashion. It is likely to have been carved by one of the court sculptors working at Versailles, and Jean Raon is the most probable candidate. Raon was the author of a set of six hermed busts inspired by the Antique which are now at the Château de Thoiry, one of which is signed. Amongst this set of busts is a model of a young faun who wears a crown of ivy and a goatskin around his shoulders and can be compared with the present bust both for the modelling and in the playful character conveyed in the faun's expression.

Jean Raon entered the Académie Royale in 1666, the same year in which he was sent by the king to Rome along with Jean-Jacques Clérion and François Lespingola to study at the French Academy. Raon was appointed to oversee the antiquities which entered France for the royal collection – a position which would have greatly embellished his understanding of classical sculpture.

The famous compositions by Raon and his son are in herm form, and the present marble is unusual in that it is represented as a true bust.

RELATED LITERATURE

L. Murat and R. Scherzen, *Les Grandes Demeures de France*, Paris 1991, p. 334

F. Souchal, *French Sculptors of the 17th and 18th Centuries: The Reign of Louis XIV,* Oxford 1981–93, vols. III–IV, pp. 212–28, illus. p. 224, and pp. 180–85

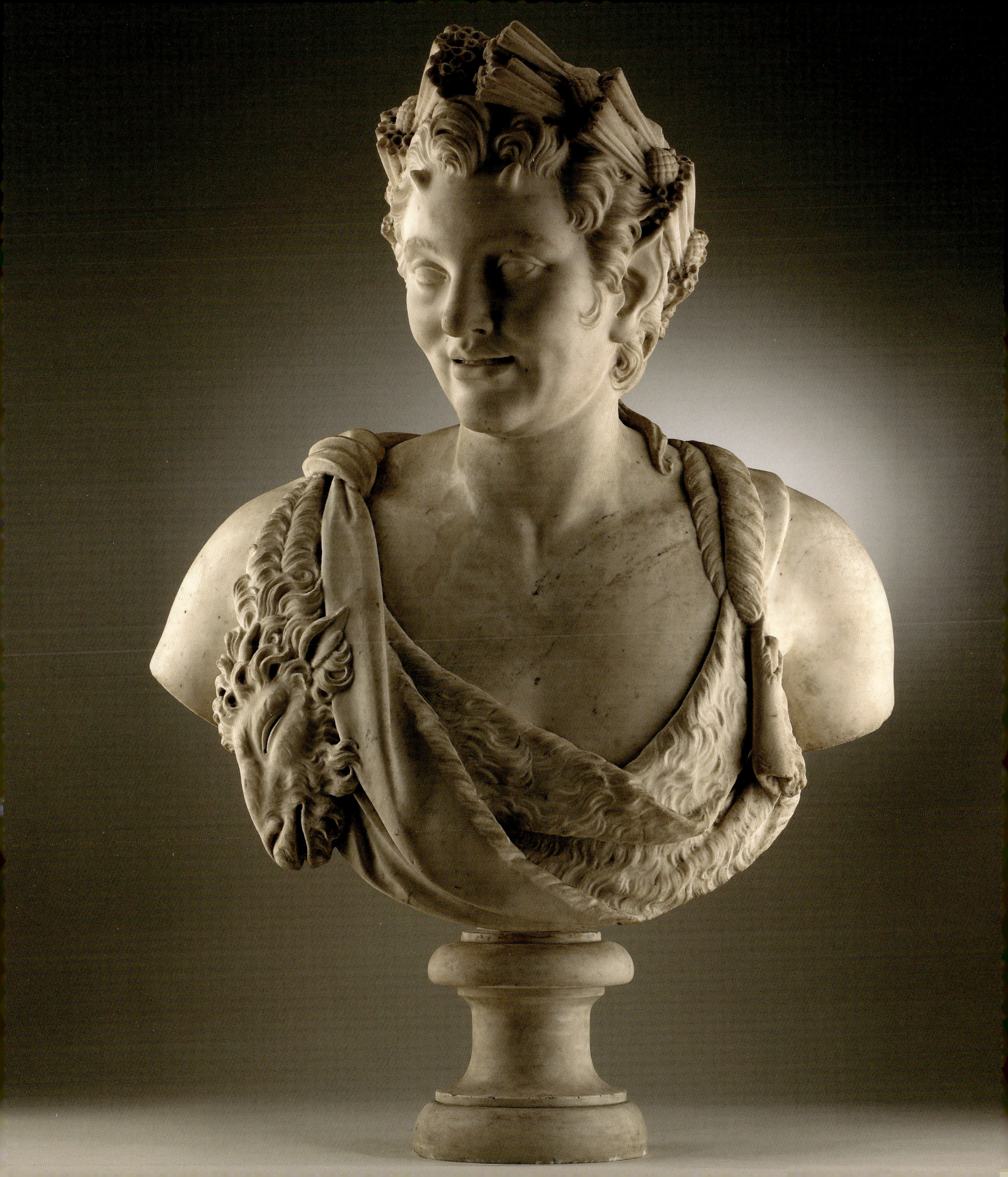

21. FRENCH, 17th century

possibly cast by MICHEL ANGUIER (1612–1686)

The Farnese Flora

Bronze, rich brown patina with traces of red lacquer

19 ¾ in. (50 cm) high

PROVENANCE: Tissington Hall, near Ashbourne, Derbyshire, probably acquired by Sir William Fitzherbert, 1st Bt, whilst on the Grand Tour, *c.* 1768–69

This very fine and beautifully preserved, elegant and feminine bronze model of the famous Farnese *Flora* was cast in France during the reign of the Sun King, Louis XIV. The Farnese *Flora* was one of the most sought-after antique statues that captured the imagination of prestigious collectors from the sixteenth century to the Neoclassical period. The main torso was drawn by Marten van Heemskerk whilst he was in Rome between 1532 and 1536, making studies of all the most eminent antique sculptures.

The high regard in which ancient Greek and Roman statues were held by the upper echelons of French society during the seventeenth century is proven by the multitude of statuary that was carved for most of the major gardens in France, including the Tuileries, Paris, and the Château de Versailles.

This bronze has an important provenance, having been bought by William Fitzherbert IV, 1st Bt, whilst on his Grand Tour with his friend and neighbour William Cavendish, 5th Duke of Devonshire, in 1768–69.

RELATED EXAMPLE

An identical cast of this model is held by the Louvre, Paris, no. OA 6346, which bears the Louis XIV inv. no. 322; illustrated in *Les Bronzes de la Couronne*, exh. cat., Musée du Louvre, Paris, 1999, p. 182, no. 322

RELATED LITERATURE

F. Souchal, *French Sculptors of the 17th and 18th Centuries: The Reign of Louis XIV,* Oxford 1981–93, vol. III, p. 217, pl. 24

'Tissington Hall, Derbyshire, The Seat of Hugo Meynell Fitzherbert, Bt.', *Country Life*, 11 March 1911, p. 345; illustrated *in situ* in the drawing-room

H.A. Tipping, *Tissington Hall, English Homes Period III, Late Tudor and Early Stuart 1558–1649,* London 1927, vol. II, p. 196, fig. 237

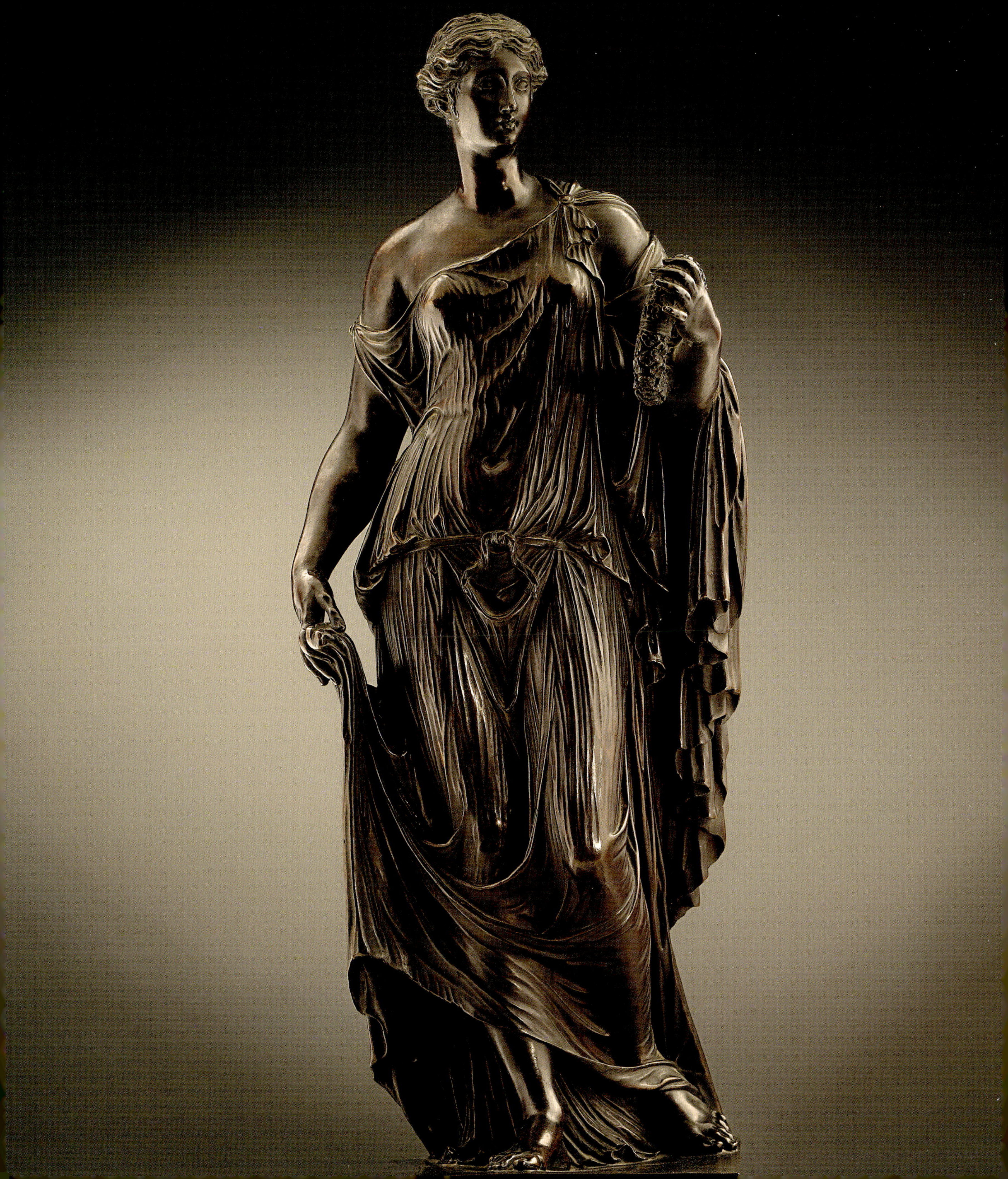

22. ETIENNE LE HONGRE (1628–1690)

(attributed to)

Equestrian Portrait of King Louis XIV of France

Bronze

14 in. (33 cm) high

PROVENANCE: The Hon. Mrs Dorothy Rose Burns (d. 1985), daughter of Lord Duveen of Millbank; private collection, United Kingdom

Since antiquity the equestrian monument has been considered one of the most symbolically potent and artistically challenging forms of sculptural commemoration. Whether it be a peaceful image of a king guiding a calmly advancing horse, or a more dramatic image of a ruler controlling a rearing steed, for centuries the equestrian monument has served as a symbol of an assured leader in control of the future.

The famous bronze statue of Marcus Aurelius (166–180 AD; Capitoline Museum, Rome) is the sole survivor of this genre from ancient Roman times and has always been one of the eternal city's most treasured antiquities. It served as both a model and a touchstone for later artists tackling the technical challenges of the form, which requires that the enormous weight of horse and rider be supported on the rather slender supporting elements of the horse's legs. Italy's most famous artists of the Renaissance – Donatello, Verrocchio, Leonardo, Michelangelo and Giambologna – designed equestrian monuments for leaders ranging from Italian *condottieri* and Medici dukes to the kings of France, England and Spain.

Inspired by this tradition, in 1665 King Louis XIV of France commissioned his own equestrian statue from Italy's foremost artist, Gianlorenzo Bernini. When Bernini's marble statue of Louis XIV on a rearing horse finally arrived in Paris twenty years later, it was rejected; it was transformed by the sculptor François Girardon into an image of *Marcus Curtius throwing Himself into the Flames* and was displayed in a remote corner of the gardens of Versailles. It certainly is no coincidence that, beginning in the same year, a series of equestrian monuments was planned to promote the image of the King in the provinces. France's most important sculptors were entrusted with these prestigious commissions, among them François Girardon for the Place Louis-le-Grand (now the Place Vendôme) in Paris, Antoine Coysevox for the city of Rennes, Pierre Mazeline and Simon Hurtrelle for Montpellier, Martin Desjardins for Lyons, and Etienne Le Hongre for Dijon.

As discussed by Michel Martin in his extensive study of the equestrian monuments of King Louis XIV, the general design all of the monuments was laid out by Jules-Hardouin Mansart, then the most important architect at the royal court. According to Martin, Mansart oversaw the projects from their inception in 1685 until his death in 1708. He provided preparatory drawings for the sculptors to use as guidelines for their work, but allowed them to alter certain details of the designs as long as the final project maintained the proper decorum.

All of the designs were based upon the equestrian statue of Marcus Aurelius, of which there was a plaster cast in the courtyard of the Louvre. Like Marcus Aurelius, Louis XIV was shown riding a trotting horse without stirrups, in the antique manner. With the exception of his voluminous *perruque*, the ruler was also dressed *all'antica*, wearing a cuirass and sandals, with a billowing mantle clasped at the shoulder.

All of the large-scale equestrian monuments of Louis XIV were destroyed during the French Revolution, but the designs of many are known from surviving drawings, engravings, models and reductions. While the present group does not appear to correspond exactly to any

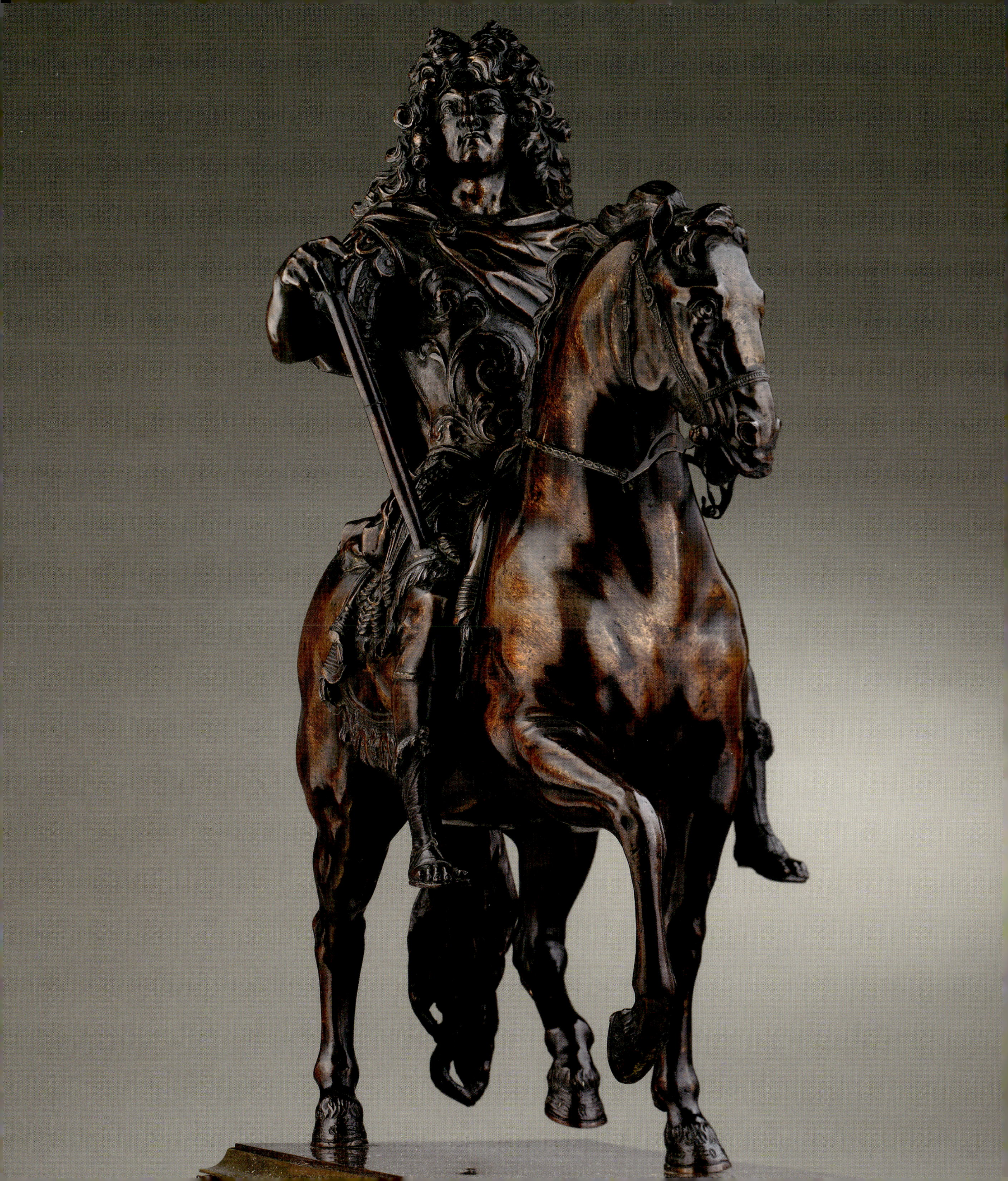

of the known monuments as finally executed, it is closely related to preparatory works for at least two projects – Martin Desjardins's monument for the Place Bellecour in Lyons, and Etienne Le Hongre's monument for the Place Royale in Dijon, both commissioned in 1686.

Two of Mansart's designs for the monument at Lyons are closely comparable to the present work. In both drawings the king is shown in the same pose as in our bronze statuette: he holds the reins with his left hand, while resting the end of a baton on his right thigh and looking out over his right shoulder. The position of the horse is also comparable. In both drawings the horse's head is turned to the left. Also similar is the placement of the horse's legs, with one foreleg raised while the tip of the opposite rear hoof rests lightly on the ground (in the sculpture, however, the rear hoof is raised slightly off the ground). One of the Lyons drawings shows the horse with the right foreleg raised as in our bronze. The Lyons monument as finally executed by Desjardins, however, differed from Mansart's drawings and from our bronze statuette in several ways. As attested by Benoît and Jean Audran's 1720 engraving of the Lyons monument *in situ* (Martin 1986, fig. 78) and several surviving bronze reductions from the Desjardins workshop (Martin 1986, figs. 79–91), in the Lyons monument the king looked out over his left shoulder, away from the baton in his right hand, and was seated on a saddlecloth decorated with a distinctive sunburst, while his horse advanced with its left foreleg. These differences suggest that, despite its similarities to the designs for it, the present bronze group was not produced in connection with Desjardins's Lyons monument.

Two drawings by Mansart also survive for the equestrian statue of Louis XIV by Etienne Le Hongre, formerly at the Place Royale in Dijon. These, too, are comparable to the present bronze. The first depicts the monument in profile and shows the king raising his baton and looking straight ahead, while the horse's right foreleg is lifted as in our group. The second shows the monument head on, with the king resting the end of the baton against his right thigh while his horse raises its right foreleg, as in the present bronze. The latter drawing differs, however, in that the king looks out over his left shoulder. The pose of our statuette, therefore, reflects a combination of the two designs shown in Mansart's drawings for Dijon.

Martin lists one plaster and seven bronze statuettes of varying quality (Martin 1986, pp. 162–163, figs. 97–102) that correspond to Mansart's designs for Dijon and are believed to record the monument as finally executed by Le Hongre. The present bronze differs from those reductions in one significant way: the king looks out over his right shoulder rather than his left. In spite of this difference, however, our group corresponds more closely to the bronze reductions associated with Le Hongre's Dijon monument than to any other statuettes of the king's equestrian monuments. Significant points of comparison include the treatment of the horse's mane and tail, which hangs freely; the arrangement of the king's cloak, which is secured by a clasp at the right shoulder and blown by the wind over his left upper arm, settling into a backwards s-curve where it meets the saddle blanket; the form of the ornamented flaps on the skirt, which split down the middle and terminate in two corkscrew curls; the type of saddle blanket with tasselled, undulating edges decorated with fleurs-de-lis; the manner in which the fabric sags and crumples under the king's weight; and the inclusion of a sword, although its exact placement differs slightly among the statuettes.

Martin considers the varying quality, details and dimensions (36–38 cm high) of the seven bronze statuettes associated with the Dijon monument and concludes that they were produced by more than one source, with the finest examples, such as those formerly in the Straus and Meyer collections (Martin 1986, figs. 97 and 100, respectively), originating in Le Hongre's own workshop, where they may have been produced as gifts for important patrons. Martin believes that the statuettes of lesser quality probably date to the time of the statue's inauguration in 1725, or slightly thereafter. The quality of the present group suggests that it is a product of Le Hongre's workshop, and the fact that it differs slightly from the others, in that the king looks towards his right rather than his left, suggests that it may record an earlier model by Le

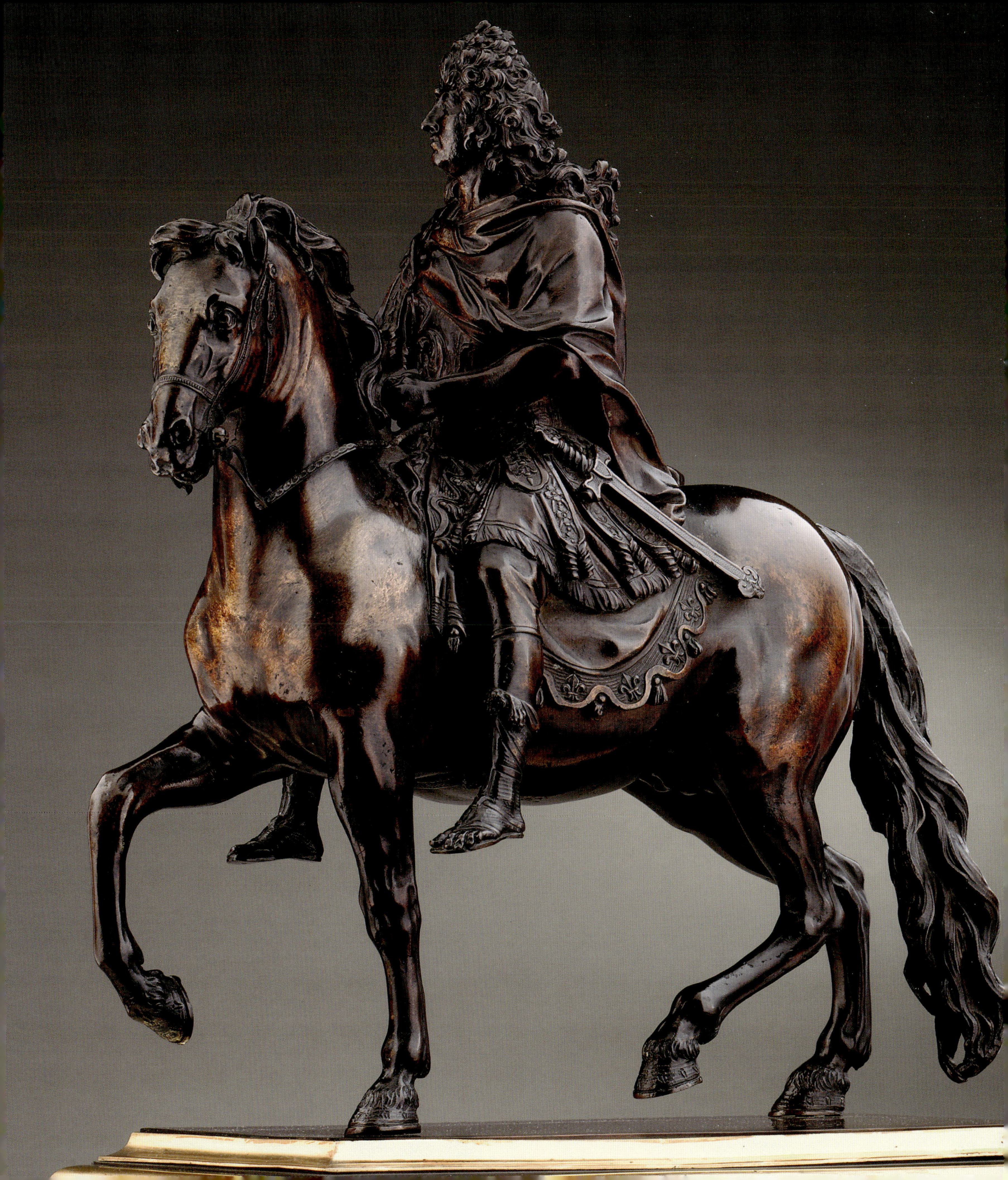

Hongre for the Dijon monument, made before he had settled on the final composition. The present group appears to be the only surviving example of this particular model.

While no written record of such a model from Le Hongre's workshop is known, the practice of artists or members of their workshops casting reductions after the master's models was not unusual at this time. Girardon himself cast and signed a reduced version of his equestrian monument for the Place Louis-le-Grand, now in the Louvre. Furthermore, models of Desjardins's monument for Lyons are recorded in the posthumous inventory of the artist's studio and were used by his descendants to cast bronze statuettes. One such reduction survives, with its moulding vents intact, in the Museum of Decorative Arts, Copenhagen.

Etienne Le Hongre's monument to Louis XIV for the Place Royale of Dijon was commissioned in 1686 by the États de Bourgogne, led by the Prince of Condé, for whom the artist had already worked on several occasions. Le Hongre completed the full-scale model shortly before his death in 1690, and the statue was cast in two separate pieces by two of his students, Roger Schabol and François Aubry. Although completed and ready for transport in 1692, the process of transferring the sculpture from Paris to Dijon was a complicated affair that took twenty-nine years. The monument arrived in 1721 and was finally inaugurated in 1725. Its appearance *in situ* is recorded in a drawing and two engravings by Lallemand and Antoine (Martin 1986, figs. 94–96; for discussion of the monument's history, see pp. 157–64).

Le Hongre's Dijon project was not the artist's first encounter with a royal equestrian statue. In 1673, in the courtyard at the Academy in Paris, he exhibited a maquette of King Louis XIV mounted on a pre-existing bronze horse that had been made by the Chaligny brothers in 1621 for the city of Nancy as part of a never-completed monument to Duke Charles III of Lorraine. When Louis XIV occupied Nancy in 1670 he had the horse transferred to Paris to be 'completed' by Le Hongre. Le Hongre's effigy was probably made in plaster or stucco, as it was described a few years later as already having suffered from the ravages of time.

Etienne Le Hongre was from a large artistic family. His father was a master-joiner in Paris who worked in Notre-Dame and at the Louvre and maintained friendships with many well-known artists and architects, such as François Mansart (the great uncle of Jules-Hardouin Mansart), Louis Le Vau, Simon Vouet and Jacques Sarazin, all of whom became godparents of Etienne or one of his eight siblings. Etienne trained with the sculptor Jacques Sarazin in Paris before travelling to Rome in 1653 with a grant from the king. In 1663 he was approved by the Académie Royale de Peinture et de Sculpture, and was accepted as a full member in 1667. In 1687 Le Hongre became assistant rector and was granted lodgings in the Louvre. From 1663 he was involved in the royal works of Louis XIV and created numerous works for the château and gardens at Versailles, and for the châteaux of Val, Clagny and Marly. In addition to his work for the king, Le Hongre also received commissions to create works for many important private patrons in Paris and elsewhere, such as Louis de Cossé, Duke of Brissac; Louis Potier, Marquis of Gesvres; Jacques Souvré de Courtenvaux, Grand Prior of the Order of the Knights of Malta; the Condé family; and Anne-Marie-Louise d'Orléans, Duchess of Montpensier.

J.S.

RELATED LITERATURE

S.A. Callisen, 'The Equestrian Statue of Louis XIV in Dijon', *Art Bulletin*, XXIII, 1941, pp. 131–46

L. Camins, *Glorious Horsemen: Equestrian Art in Europe, 1500–1800*, exh. cat., Museum of Fine Arts, Springfield, MA (and tour), 1981–82, esp. pp. 33–37

S. Lami, *Dictionnaire des Sculpteurs de l'Ecole francaise sous le regne de Louis XIV*, Paris 1906, pp. 306–12

M. Martin, *Les Monuments équestres de Louis XIV: Un grand enterprise de propagande monarchique*, Paris 1986

P. Quarre, 'La statue equestre de Louis XIV sur la Place royale', *Mémoires de la Commission des Antiquités du Département de la Cote d'Or*, XXV, 1959–62, pp. 89–92

F. Souchal, *French Sculptors of the 17th and 18th Centuries: The Reign of Louis XIV,* Oxford 1981–93, vol. II, pp. 300–31

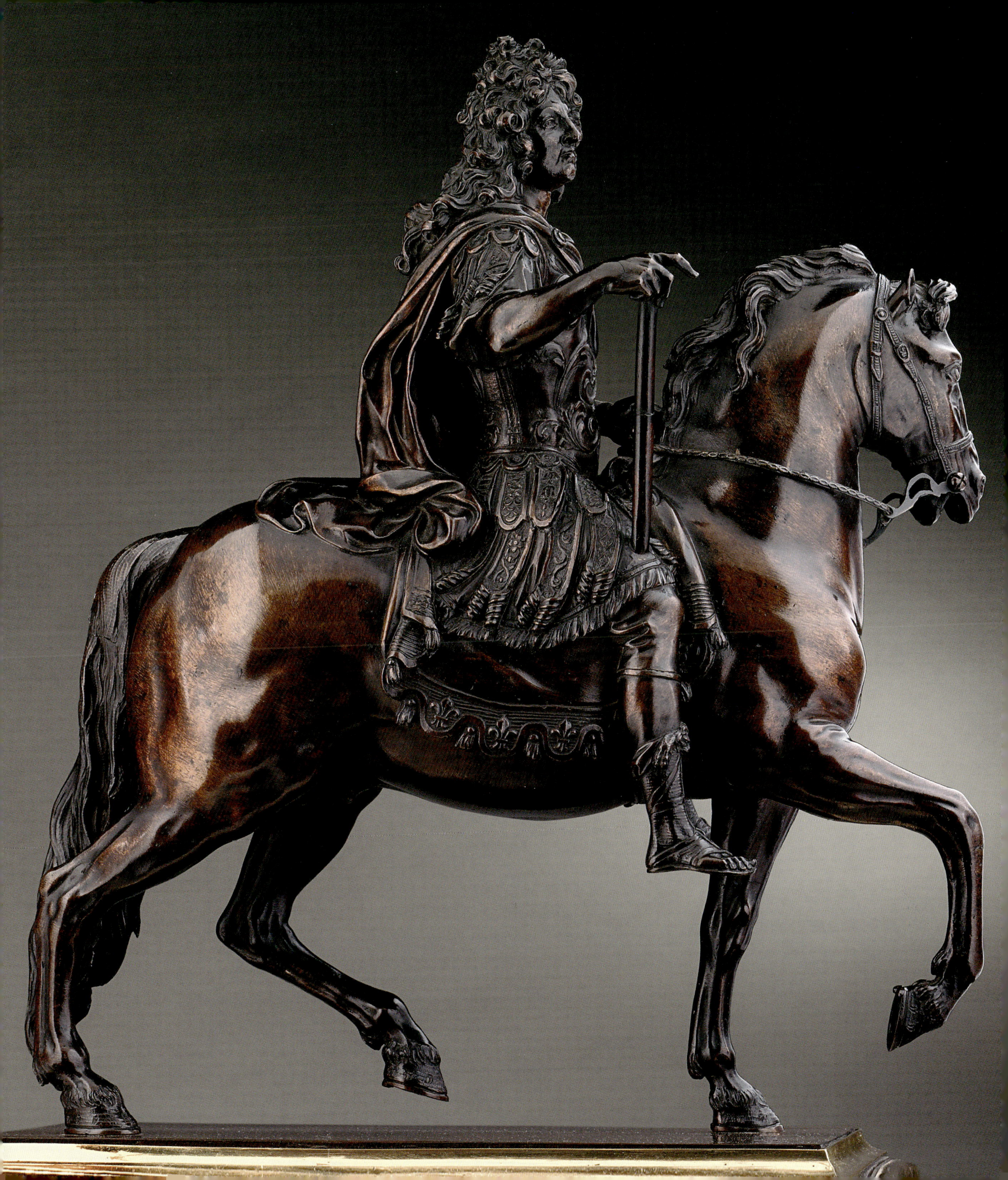

23. ENGLISH SCHOOL, 18th century

Relief Portrait of Henry Purcell (*c.* 1658–1695)

White marble

7 1/8 in. (18 cm) high, 5 1/2 in. (14 cm) wide

This fine portrait relief dating from the early eighteenth century depicts Henry Purcell, the most important of England's composers working at the end of the seventeenth century. Henry was the son of Henry Purcell senior, who was a Gentleman of the Chapel Royal and who sang at the Coronation of Charles II. He went on to be appointed to the prestigious position of Organist at Westminster Abbey and also the Chapel Royal. Purcell was a prolific composer of both secular and sacred music, having arranged the first *Te Deum* in England. Although he died at a young age, he went on to influence later generations of composers – most notably, in the twentieth century, Benjamin Britten and Michael Nyman.

There are several extant portrait reliefs of this size and period, representing grandiose sitters of the later seventeenth and early eighteenth century, but they are almost all in boxwood. Although the sculptor of the present relief is anonymous for the moment, it should be noted that it bears an affinity to the work of the great ivory carver David le Marchand.

RELATED EXAMPLE

A relief of similar size and depicting the same sitter adorned with a laurel wreath can be found in the collections of the Victoria and Albert Museum, London, inv. no. A5.1988.

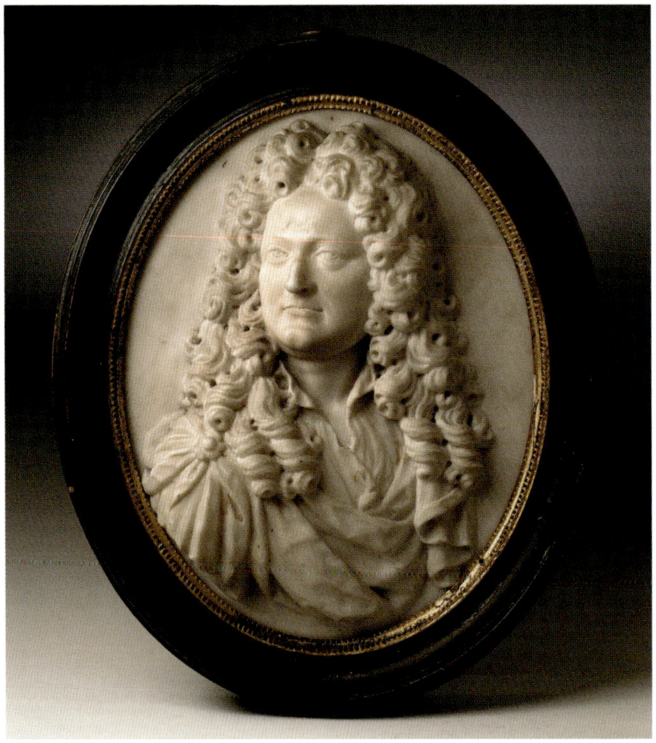

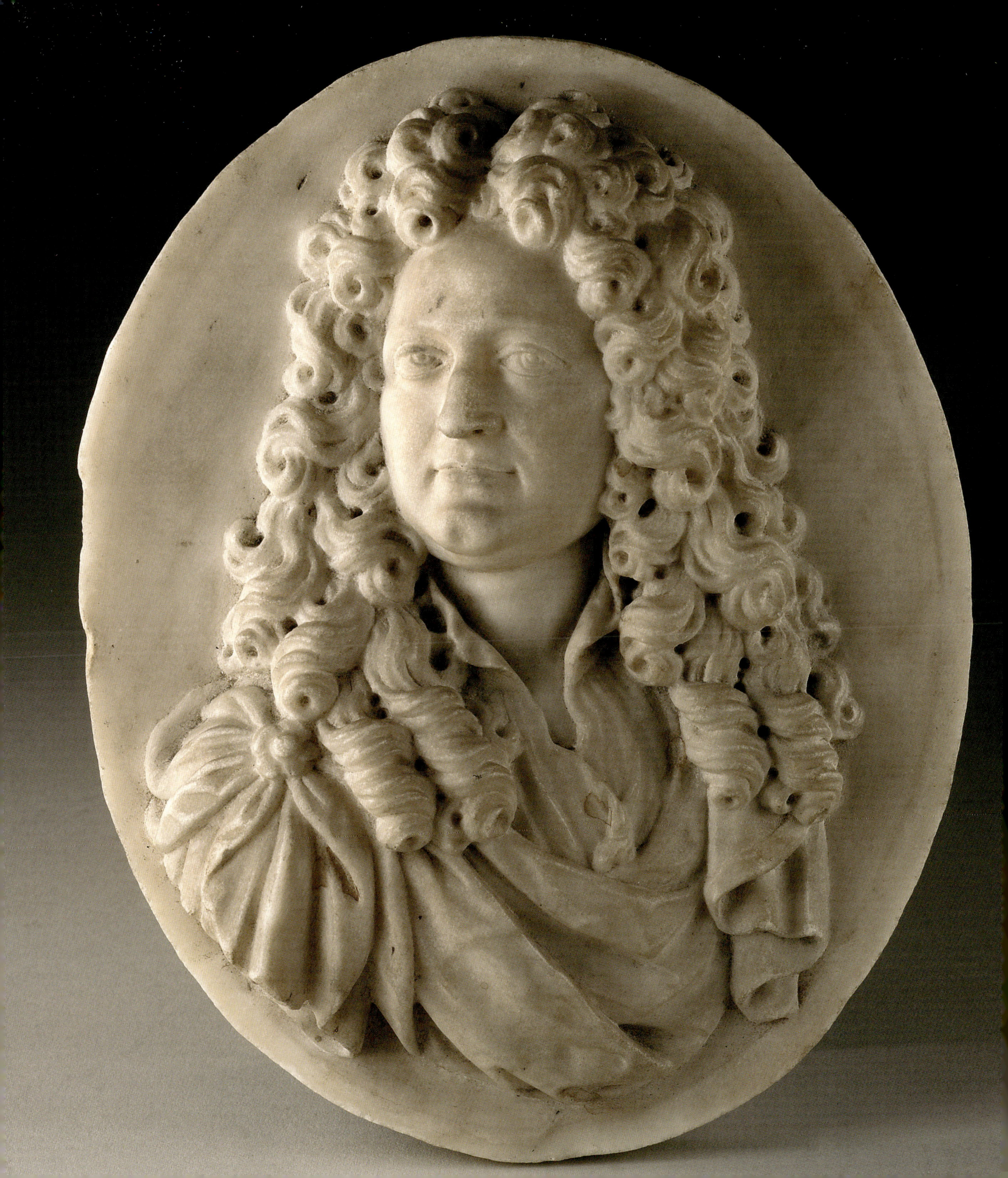

24. JAN CLAUDIUS DE COCK (1667–1735)

A Pair of Figures representing Air and Fire

Both signed: *J.C. de Cock*

Inscribed: *AYER* and *IGNIS*

Terracotta

10 5/8 in. (27 cm) high (*Air*) and 10 1/4 in. (26 cm) high (*Fire*)

Jan Claudius de Cock joined the Antwerp Guild in 1688/89, where he quickly excelled in his craft and became an independent master. His principal influences came from other prominent Flemish sculptors, such as François Duquesnoy and Artus Quellinus the Elder. The legacy of Duquesnoy is evident in de Cock's adoption of the three-quarter profile and the undulating hair in the model of *Air*. Whilst de Cock did produce several notable sculptures of religious inspiration, he is more widely recognized for his intimate renditions of children that personify allegories, in both marble and terracotta.

Seen here is a previously unrecorded pair of terracottas showing a young European boy holding aloft a chameleon whilst being supported by billowing clouds; he represents Air. His counterpart, a young Moorish boy, who holds an exotic fruit, possibly a pomegranate, stands before a flaming urn; he represents Fire. No known marbles for these *modelli* exist, but it would be feasible that they represented two of the continents, namely Europe and Africa, giving the models a dual symbolism.

Inspired by Italian prototypes – popular in Northern Europe during the late seventeenth and eighteenth centuries – these slightly chubby animated figures captured in playful stances are typical of de Cock's lively style.

Although both the models are signed and inscribed they are not dated. However, if we compare these terracottas with the well-known marble by de Cock held by the Rijksmuseum, *Boy with Mural Crown: Africa,* which is dated 1704, a date of *c.* 1705 would make stylistic and chronological sense.

RELATED LITERATURE

J. Leeuwenberg and W. Halsema-Kubes, *Beeldhouwkunst in het Rijksmuseum*, Amsterdam 1973, pp. 253–54, no. 339A

Sculpture and Works of Art, exh. cat., Thomas Agnew & Sons Ltd., London, 10 October–11 December 1981, no. 8

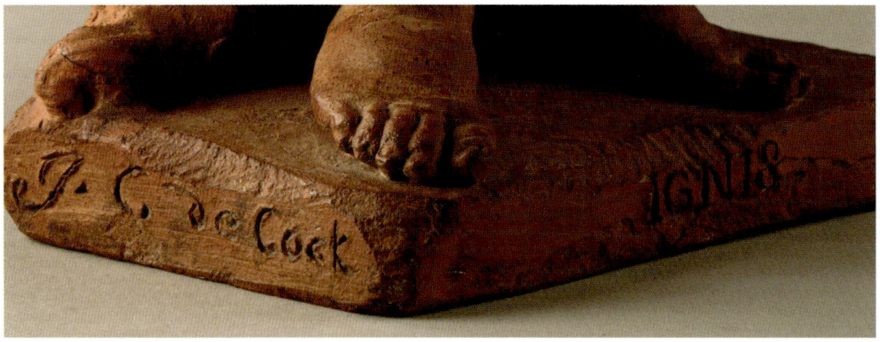

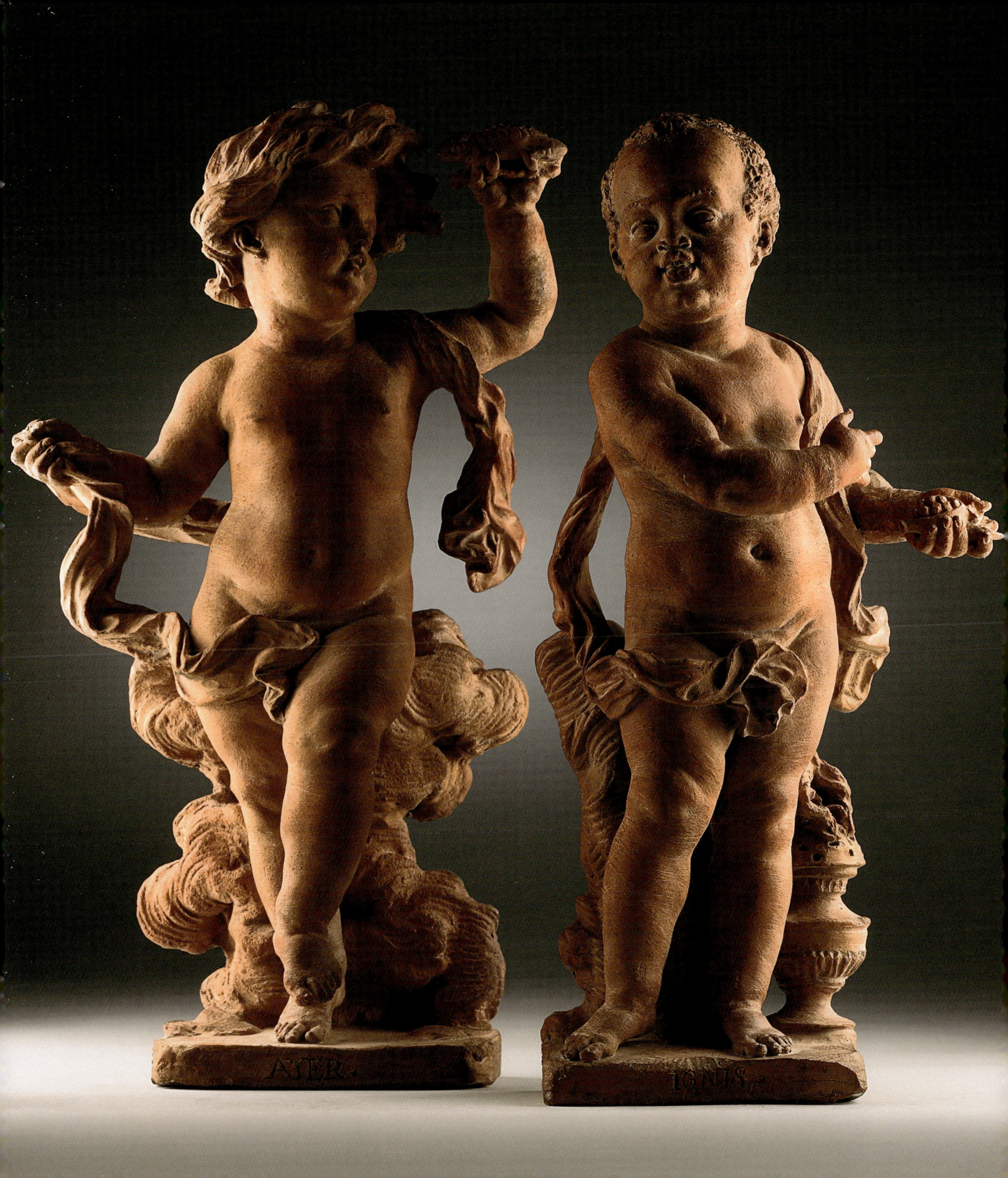
AYER
IGNIS

25. GIOVANNI GIULIANI (1663–1744)

A Pair of Putti

White marble

8 1/4 in. (21 cm) high

Giovanni Giuliani began his training in Venice, but by 1680 we know that he was working in Munich with Andreas Faistenberger. In 1689 he moved to Vienna and began working for the Viennese aristocracy, establishing himself as the most important Italian sculptor working in the later Baroque style in and around the city. His vibrant and decorative manner was highly successful and very appealing to the taste of collectors during the late seventeenth and early eighteenth centuries. He secured appointments to several highly important patrons, such as Prince Eugene of Austria and the Prince of Liechtenstein, both of whom used him to supply sculptures for both the interiors and the gardens at the Winterpalais on the Himmelpfortgasse and for the Liechtenstein palaces at Rossau and Vienna, and the Kauntiz Palace in Slavkov, Moravia, respectively.

Although there are no extant small-scale marbles to compare to the present pair of putti, a firm attribution to Giuliani can be verified by certain idiosyncratic features which characterize his series of terracotta *modelli* dating from 1739, in the Liechenstein Museum, Vienna. In these the artist depicts pairs of putti in slightly varying postures. The basic shaping of the features is made with the same delicate rendering, producing a characteristic physiognomy common to the terracottas and the present marble examples. An idiosyncracy which seems peculiar to Giuliani is the variation he gives to the figures by using and not using voids. One of the putti has drilled nostrils and an open mouth, revealing a void inside; the other does not, and both his nostrils and his mouth are full. This individualizing of one of the figures with more pronounced features is evident in both the marble and the terracottas and we must view this, in addition to his highly recognizable animated style, as distinctive to Giuliani.

RELATED LITERATURE

J. Kraftner and L.A. Ronzoni, *Giovanni Giuliani (1664–1744)*, exh. cat., Liechtenstein Museum, Vienna, 13 March–5 October 2005, pp. 108–11, pls. 54–60

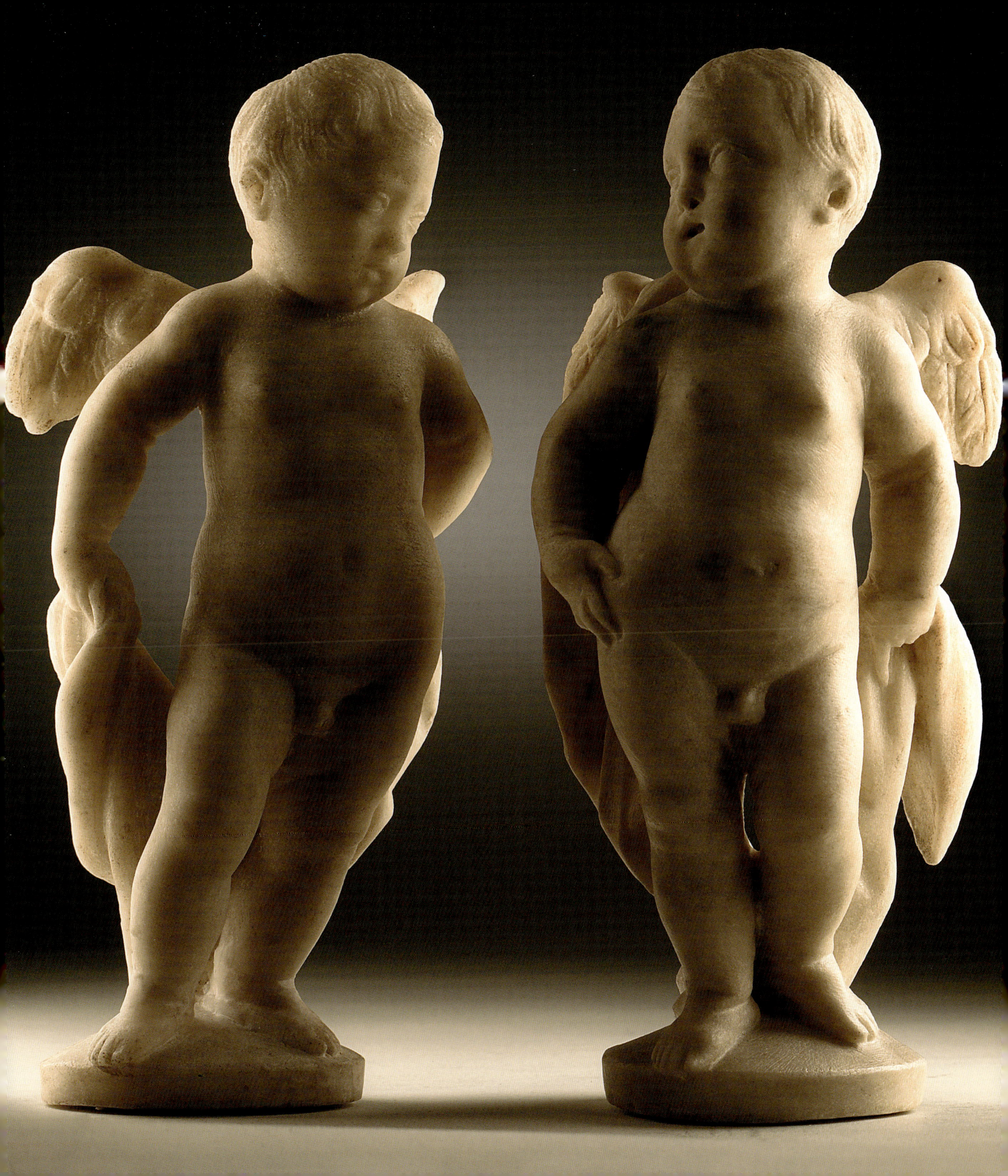

26. JEAN-PIERRE-ANTOINE TASSAERT (1727–1788)

(attributed to)

Bust of a Child

Terracotta, on mottled grey marble socle.

15 1/8 in. (38.5 cm) high

Tassaert was born in 1727 in Antwerp, the son of a sculptor. After a few years spent in London he went to Paris to train in the studio of Michel-Ange Slodtz, a fellow-countryman. He was belatedly and grudgingly received into the Académie Royale de Peinture et de Sculpture as an associate in 1769, but never worked for the court. His principal patrons were the *fermier-général* Bouret and the *contrôleur-general des finances* abbé Terray. In 1774 Tassaert was appointed court sculptor to Frederick the Great of Prussia and in 1775 moved to Berlin, where he carved a number of striking portraits, as well as further allegorical pieces. He was influenced by the sculptor Bouchardon and the painter Boucher, and was the master of the German Neoclassicist Johann Gottfried Schadow.

This bust of a charming child, probably a little boy, may be attributed convincingly to Tassaert on stylistic grounds. It compares closely with a bust of *Cupid* which he signed and dated *A. TASSAERT 1769* (illus.), as well as with putti in some other of his sculptures. The *Cupid* is an autograph excerpt made by the sculptor from his own major group *Love preparing to fire an Arrow*, in the Louvre (inv. no. 1314). There is a copy of the group in the Wallace Collection; both original and copy are initialled F.G., as is a copy of the extracted head in Waddesdon Manor. These are the initials of Messrs V. Fontaine and Ganet the Elder, who repaired the original in the Louvre in 1871 and took the opportunity of making casts from which to manufacture marble replicas (Catheu 1938). There is another copy without initials in the Jones Collection at the Victoria and Albert Museum (inv. no. 1173-1882).

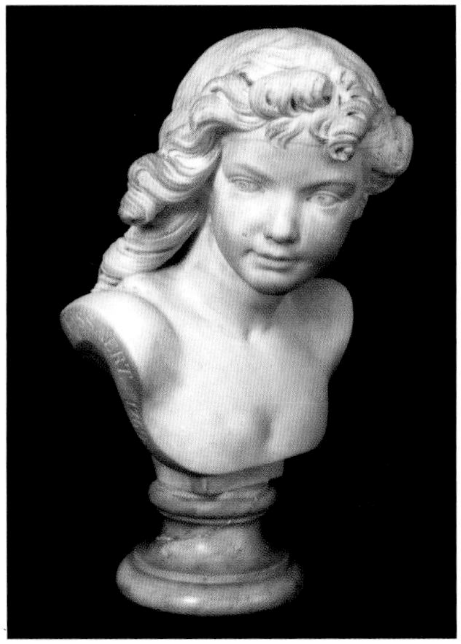

Jean-Pierre Antoine Tassaert, *Cupid*, signed and dated 1769

The pronounced eyebrows, large, wide-set, staring eyes, rounded face with its plump cheeks, and the exuberant curls of hair in the present terracotta look like a rendering of the boy in Tassaert's *Cupid* when younger. The irises are minutely rendered by little indentations made with the tip of a stylus, while the pupils have a highlight suggested by a tiny dib of clay left at the top of the incised cavity. The bouffant hair is laid on to the cranium in layers of clay that have been smoothed down with the fingers and then curled with a spatula, the individual strands being indicated with a stylus.

Children with very similar heads appear in Tassaert's major allegorical group of *Painting and Sculpture* in the National Gallery of Art, Washington, DC: the little boy representing the art of Sculpture is slightly older and has a more business-like, shorter haircut, to enable him to work unimpeded by curls. C.A.

RELATED LITERATURE

C. Avery in U. Middeldorf, *Sculptures from the Samuel H. Kress Collection: European Schools XIV–XIX Century*, Oxford 1976, pp. 104–05, figs. 176–78, 180

F. Catheu, 'L'Amour de Tassaert', *Gazette des Beaux-Arts*, vol. XIX, March 1938, pp. 185–87

T. Hodgkinson, *Sculpture, The James A. de Rothschild Collection at Waddeson Manor*, Friburg 1970, p. 72, no. 26

S. Lami, *Dictionnnaire des sculpteurs de l'école française au dix-huitième siècle*, Paris 1911, vol. II, pp. 352–56

J.G. Mann, *Wallace Collection Sculpture,* London 1931, p. 10, no. S31

L. Réau, 'Un sculpteur flamand francisé du XVIIIe siècle: Tassaert', *Revue belge d'archéologie et de l'histoire de l'art*, vol. IV, 1934, pp. 289–309

J. Turner, ed., *The Dictionary of Art*, London and New York 1996, vol. XXX, p. 353 (with further literature)

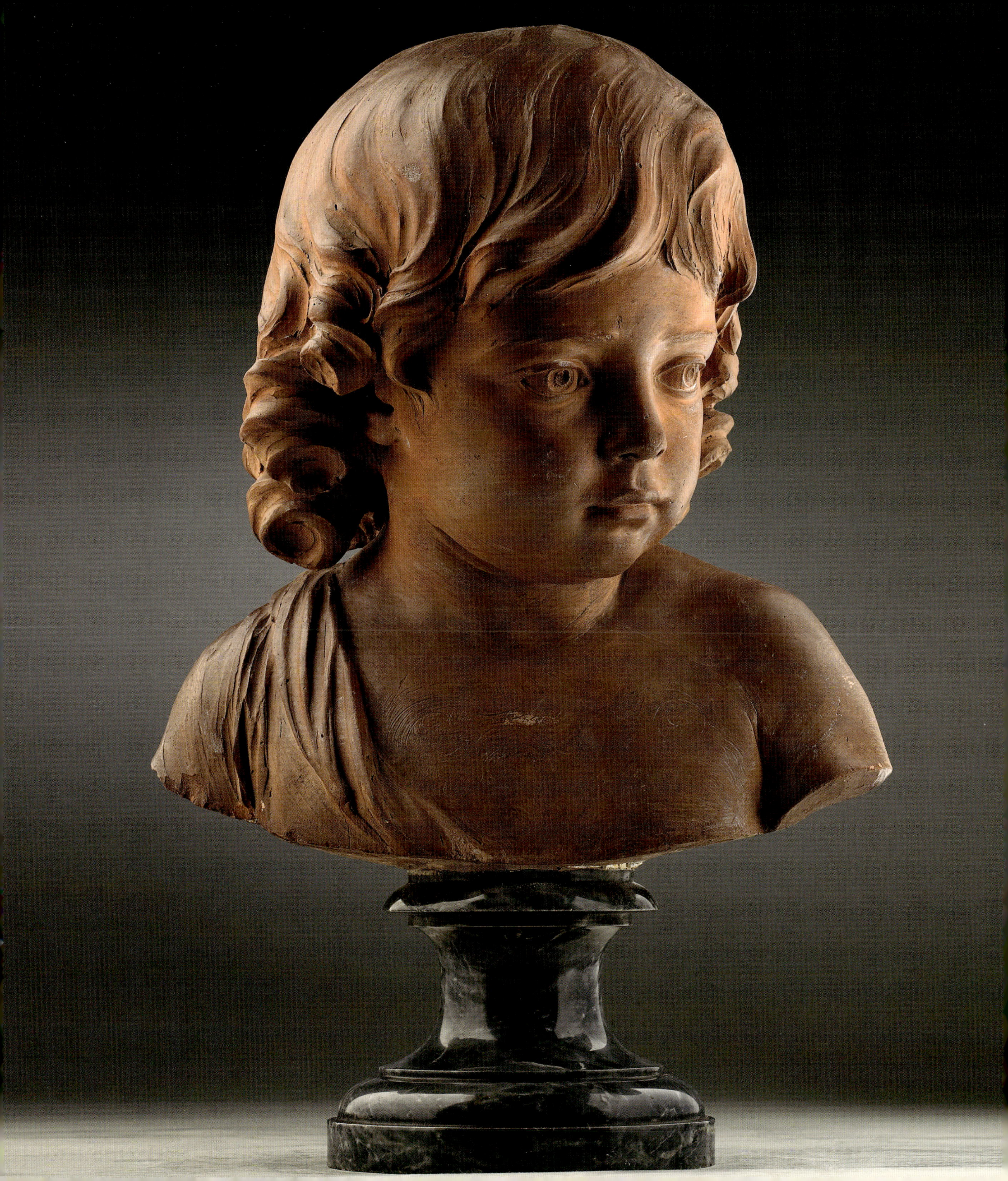

27. BARTOLOMEO CAVACEPPI (1716–1799)

(workshop of)

Bust of Faustina Minore

White marble

25 ¼ in. (64 cm) high

In Europe during the second half of the eighteenth century Cavaliere Bartolomeo Cavaceppi was the foremost sculptor working in the centuries-old tradition of restoring, reproducing and dealing in ancient marbles. He became internationally respected for his sourcing and placement of important antiquities in many of the most illustrious collections, including those of Gavin Hamilton, Thomas Jenkins, Charles Townley, William Weddell, Henry Blundell, Frederick William II of Prussia, Gustave III of Sweden and Catherine the Great of Russia. Cavaceppi travelled with the great historian Winckelmann to Northern Europe, working mostly for the Duke of Anhalt-Dessau at Schloss Wörlitz, a trip which he documented and which became both an intellectual reference and an advertisement for his art business.

Cavaceppi was an avid collector himself and upon his death he left many thousands of artefacts, including sculptures, drawings, gems and paintings. His achievements in refining the tastes of the cultured classes, most especially the English milords, should not be underestimated. The application of his enthusiasm and highly skilled business acumen to the subject of classical sculpture greatly improved understanding of the Antique, shaped art history and left a legacy of collections that today remain a wonderful academic source.

The bust presented here is a portrait of the daughter of the Emperor Antoninus Pius, Annia Galeria Faustina the Younger, who married the Emperor Marcus Aurelius in April 145 AD. The most famous ancient example of this bust was excavated at Hadrian's Villa and now resides in the Capitoline Museum, Rome. Following aristocratic protocol, and to develop their public image, gentlemen Grand Tourists would commission portraits of themselves by leading artists of the day in which they would pose surrounded by their most treasured objects. Faustina can be found depicted in several paintings from this period, most notably Pompeo Batoni's 1778 portrait of George Legge, Viscount Lewisham (Museo del Prado, Madrid, inv. no. P48).

RELATED LITERATURE

B. Allen, *El Westmorland: Recuerdos del Grand Tour*, exh. cat., Centro Cultural Las Claras, Murcia; Centro Cultural El Monte, Seville, January–March; Real Academia De Bellas Artes de San Fernando, Madrid, 2002–03, no. 49

E. Morris and M. Hopkinson, *Walker Art Gallery Foreign Catalogue*, 2 vols., Liverpool 1997, p. 292, repr. p. 429

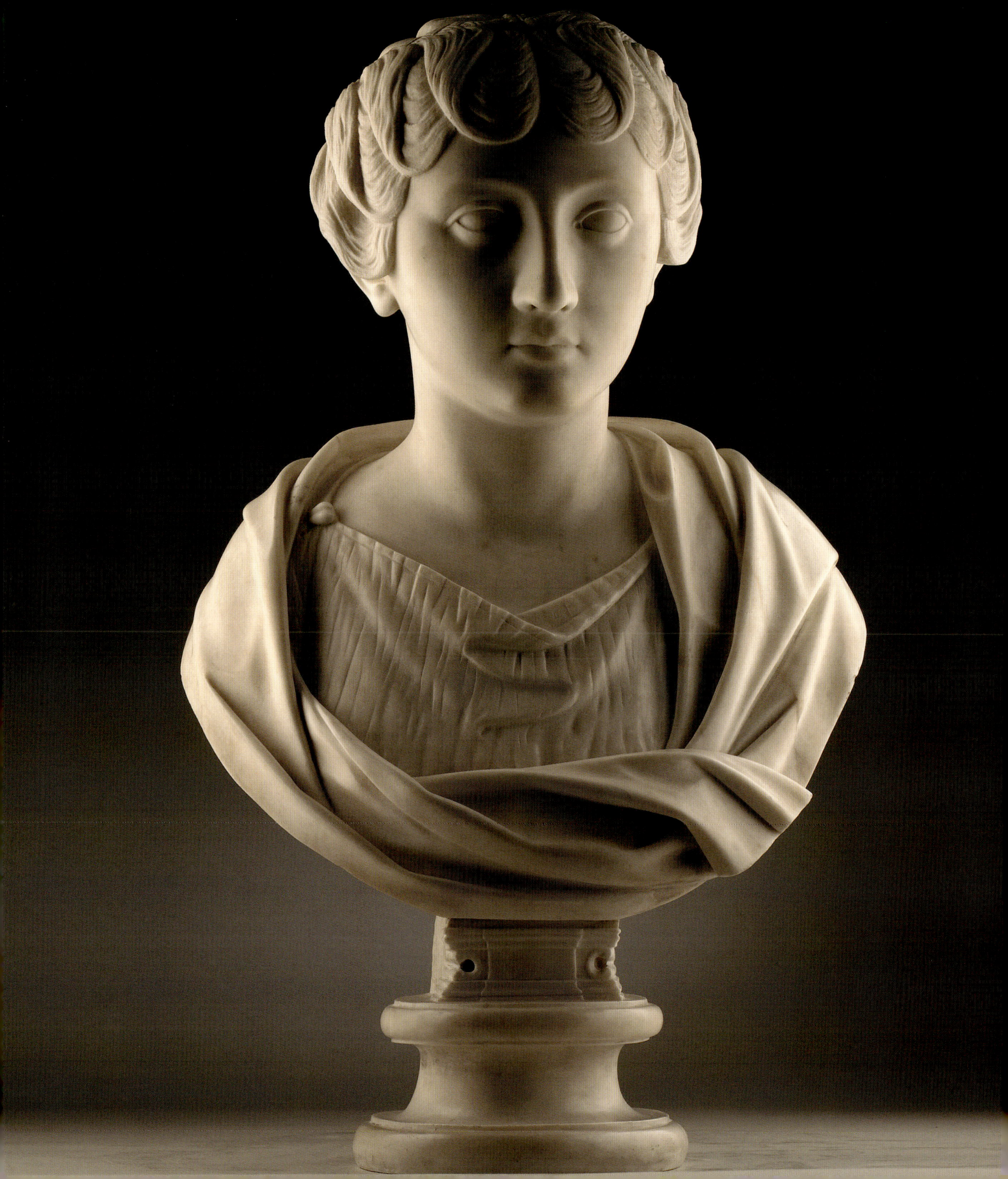

28. **ROMAN**, late 18th century

The Ludovisi Mars

Bronze, green patina

11 ¼ in. (28.5c m) high

The Ludovisi *Mars* – so called because is is first mentioned in the collection of the Ludovisi family during the first half of 1622 – is one of the most celebrated marbles of antiquity. It was counted amongst the most prestigious objects in any Roman collection, witness its prominent inclusion amongst the models which were cast in plaster and taken back to Spain for Philip IV by Velázquez in 1650. Indeed, upon its discovery in 1622 the great sculptor Gianlorenzo Bernini had himself restored the sword hilt and the putto.

RELATED LITERATURE

F. Haskell and N. Penny, *Taste and the Antique*, New Haven and London 1981, p. 260

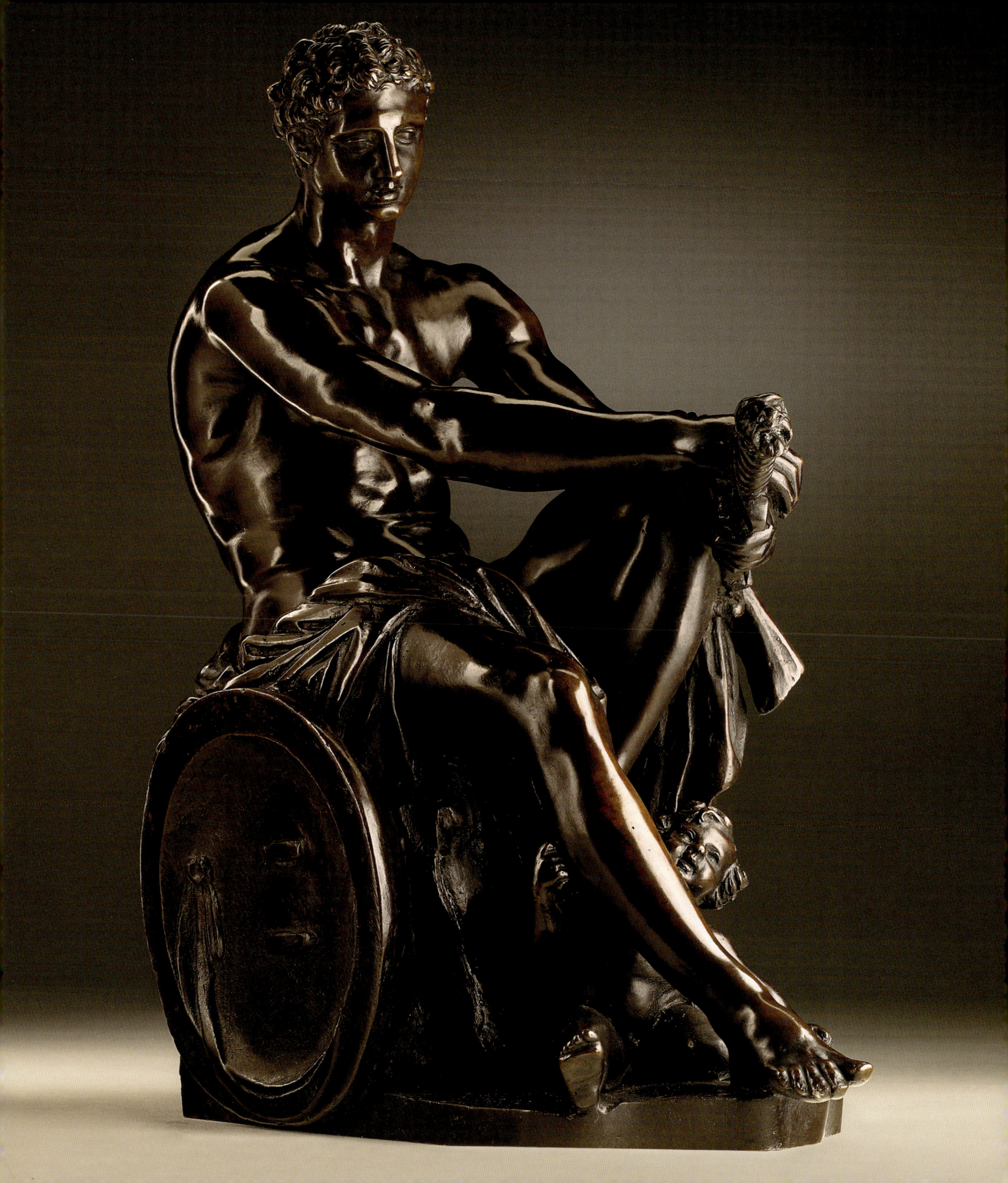

29. **ROMAN,** late 18th century

Dying Gaul

Bronze, green patina

13 in. (33 cm) wide

This fine-quality, small-scale bronze reproduces the famed life-size marble of a *Dying Gaul* or *Gladiator*, currently in the Capitoline Museum, Rome, one of the key antiquities indelibly associated with the Grand Tour of the eighteenth century. The Roman marble itself reproduced one of the figures adorning the Mausoleum at Halicarnassus, the tomb of the Greek despot Mausolus. The Capitoline marble is first mentioned as being in the Ludovisi Collection, Rome, in 1623, and by 1670 it is recorded in the inventories at a value twice that of anything else in the entire collection, illustrating the high regard in which it was held. A bronze model of the work was listed by the famous sculptor and bronze-caster Giovanni Zoffoli in his catalogue of reductions after well-known ancient models in the last quarter of the eighteenth century. The purpose of this type of bronze was mainly to adorn chimney pieces or gentlemen's desks.

RELATED LITERATURE

F. Haskell and N. Penny, *Taste and the Antique*, New Haven and London 1981, p. 224

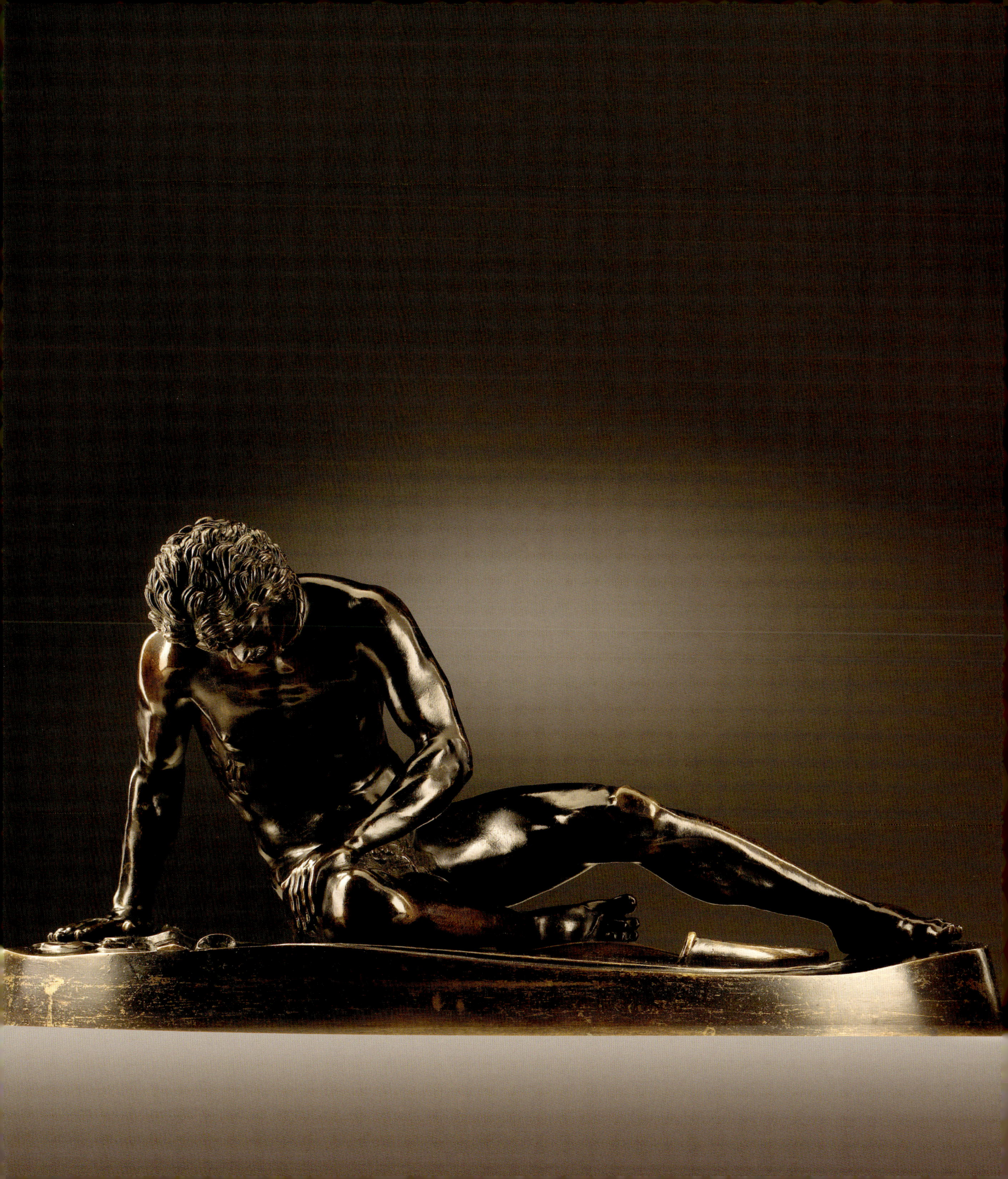

30. CARLO ALBACINI (*c.* 1770–*c.* 1810)

(circle of)

'La Zingarella'

White marble

23 ⅜ in. (59.5 cm) high

Carlo Albacini, student of the great sculptor and restorer Bartolomeo Cavaceppi, was a carver who specialized in all things antique, including both restorations of excavated marbles and contemporary creations of the most sought-after models from ancient times. He counted amongst his patrons Henry Blundell, of the famed Ince Blundell marbles, and the Dukes of Devonshire. There are examples of his works notably in the Walker Art Gallery, Liverpool.

Dating from the late eighteenth or early nineteenth century, the present bust is a superior-quality copy of one of the most recognizable antique busts, depicting a beautiful, serene, young girl whose high status is communicated through her noble, slightly raised head and confident gaze. Her *himation* is swathed around her neck and head so that only her face is showing. This image is first found in Greek terracottas of the fourth century BC; the primary version in marble is to be found in the Farnese collection at the Museo Archeologico Nazionale, Naples.

Commonly known as *La Zingarella*, the bust is generally accepted as depicting a Vestal Virgin, possibly Tuccia, who proved her doubted chastity by carrying a sieve full of water from the Tiber to the Temple of Vesta.

RELATED LITERATURE

E. Morris and M. Hopkinson, *Walker Art Gallery Foreign Catalogue*, 2 vols., Liverpool 1997, pp. 284–28, repr. pp. 411–14

B.T. Maiuri, *Museo Nazionale di Napoli,* Novara 1971, no. 32

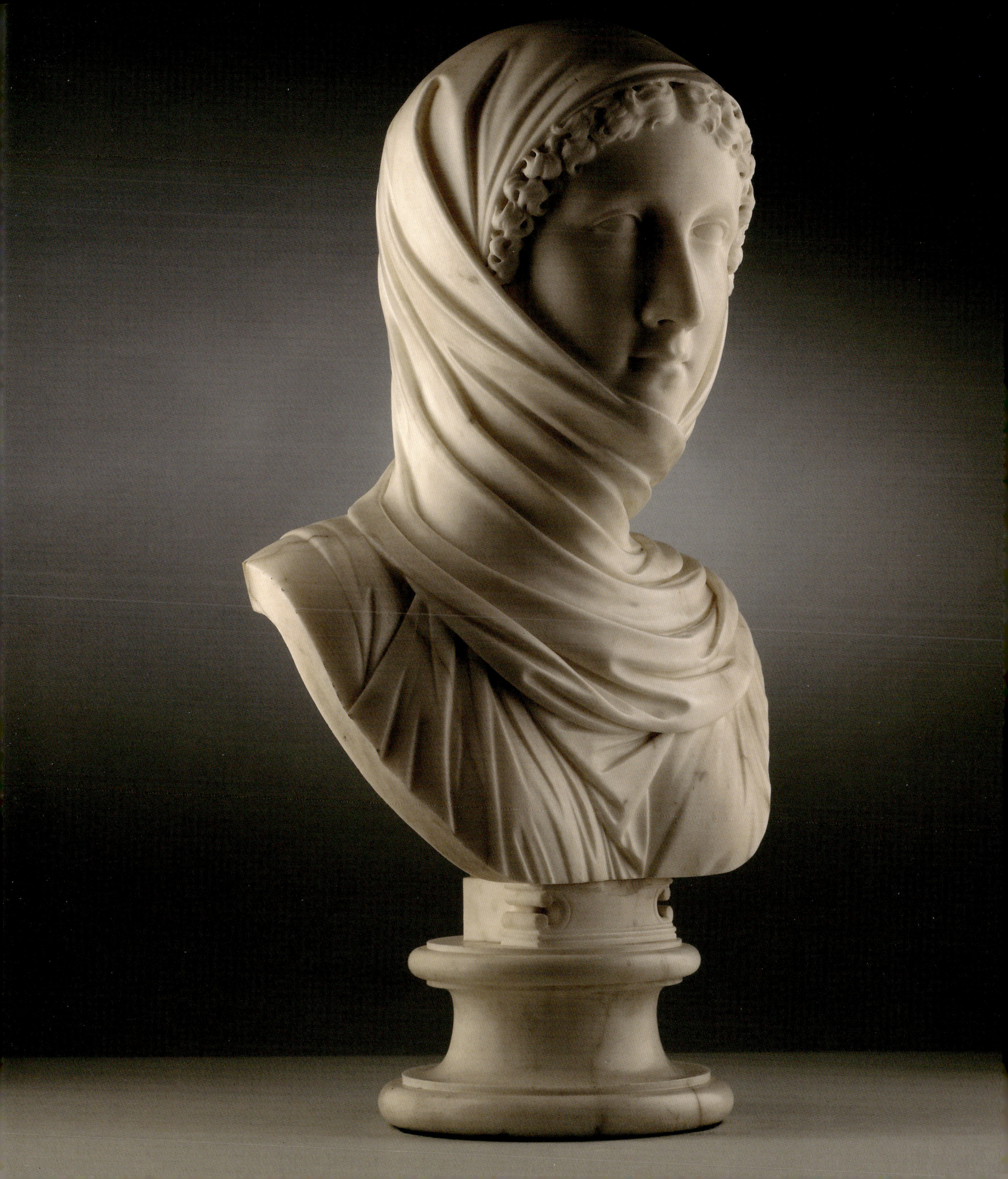

31. PIERRE PETITOT (1760–1840)

The Giustiniani Minerva

Marble

Signed: *Petitot fil. 1795*

41 ¼ in. (105 cm) high

Petitot was a pupil of François Devosges and Jean-Jacques Caffieri and went on to exhibit at the Paris Salon between 1793 and 1817. The formation of the French Empire towards the end of the eighteenth century brought a renewed fascination with ancient Rome, and with this came the dissemination of classically inspired ideals in art and culture. Petitot's style epitomizes many of the principles of the antique taste adopted by the French Empire as a way of communicating to the nation a new style representing a new regime. He is known to have made versions of antique statues and this is a beautiful example from his oeuvre.

The Giustiniani *Minerva* is one of the most recognized icons of the goddess and the present example is enriched by being signed and dated. The sculpture exudes the Roman admiration for all things Greek and is probably based on the *Athene* made by Phidias for the Parthenon. The model was celebrated throughout the eighteenth and nineteenth centuries, but seldom has it been executed in marble to such a high standard as that presented here.

RELATED LITERATURE

F. Haskell and N. Penny, *Taste and the Antique*, New Haven and London 1981, p. 269

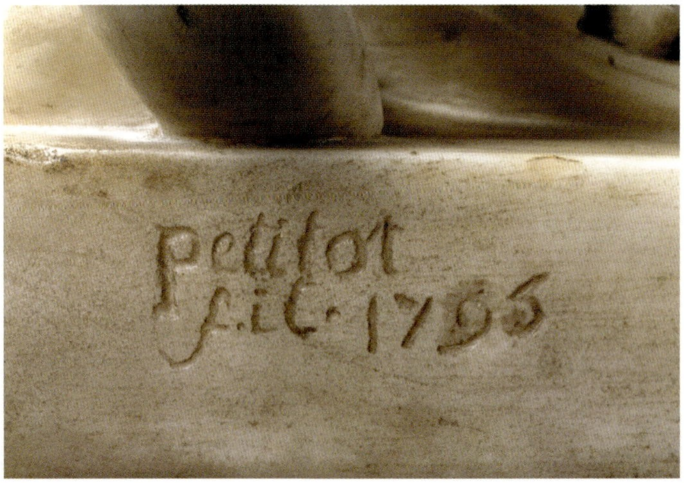

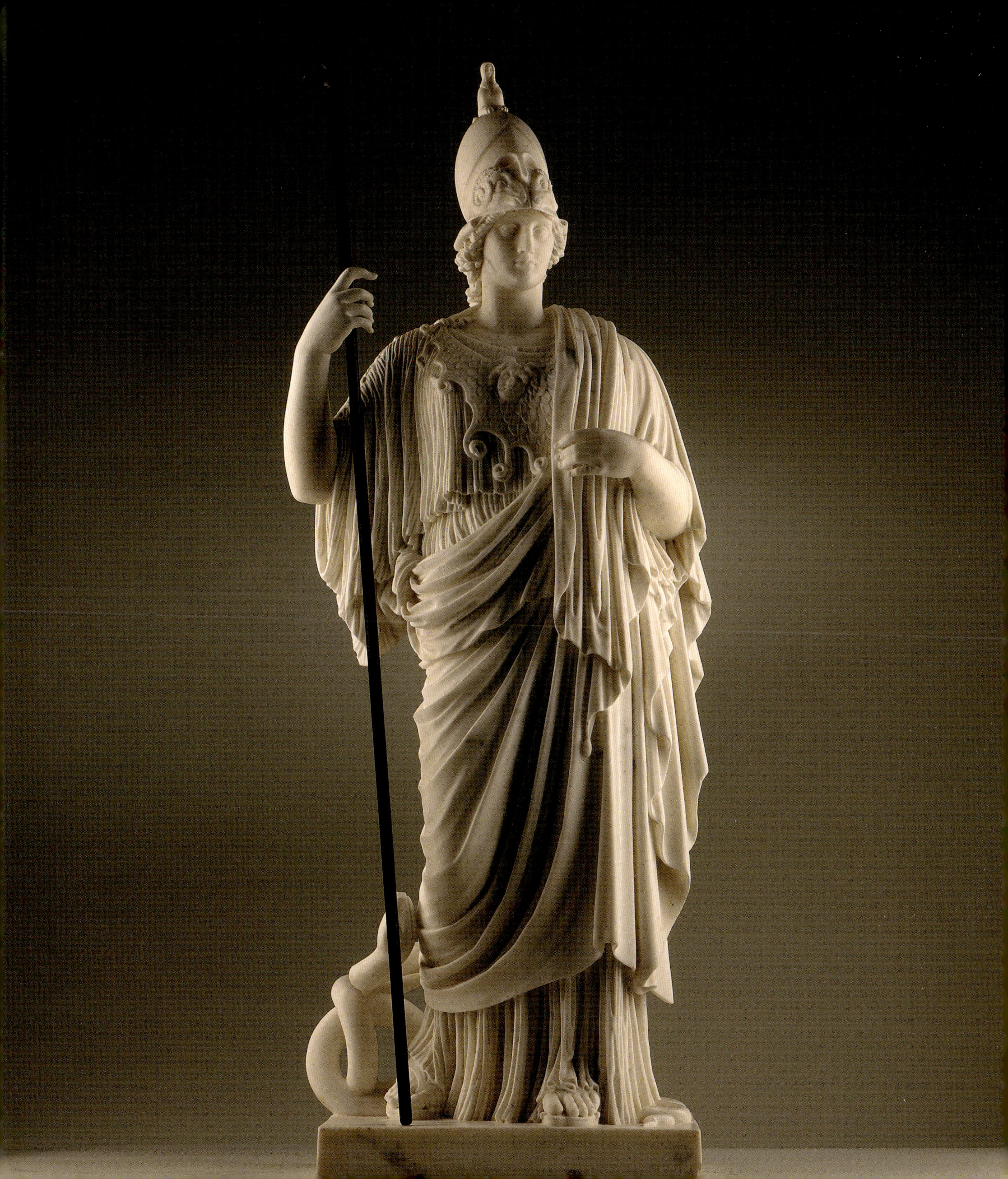

32. **GIUSEPPE BOSCHI** (active *c.* 1790–*c.* 1810)

The Laocoön

Bronze, dark green brown patina *all'antica*

Signed and inscribed: *Giuseppe. Boschi. Fece. in. Roma. 1807*

16 1/8 in. (41 cm) high, 11 1/4 in. (28. 5cm) wide

Giuseppe Boschi, together with his contemporaries Zoffoli and Righetti, was one of the chief purveyors of the classical Grand Tour taste for classical art, supplying an international clientele who were visiting the eternal city during the last decades of the eighteenth century and the beginning of nineteenth century. Contemporary documentation by Charles Heathcote Tatham describes Boschi as an "obscure" artist, although he was well known to Angelica Kauffmann and Antonio Zucchi, not to mention the most celebrated artist of his day, Antonio Canova. Boschi is known to have made small-scale bronze reductions of the most famous antiquities displayed in Rome, such as an equestrian portrait of Marcus Aurelius, a portrait bust of Cicero and a pair of busts of Achilles and Ajax.

Laocoön was a Trojan priest who warned his people against accepting the gift of a wooden horse from the Greeks. The gods, led by Minerva, whose allegiances lay with the Greeks, had Laocoön and his sons strangled by an enormous sea serpent. The sensational discovery of the monumental marble of this subject in January 1506 was made near Santa Maria Maggiore, Rome. The group was then taken by Pope Julius II to the Belvedere Courtyard in the Vatican, to reside amongst such masterpieces as the Belvedere *Apollo* and *Antinoüs*.

Upon its excavation the group was first recognized by Giuliano da Sangallo as that mentioned by Pliny in the Palace of Titus as the work of Hagesander, Polidorus and Athenodorus of Rhodes. Its immediate fame and iconic status was secured when Bramante made it the subject for copying by four of the leading sculptors of the day. The competition was won by Jacopo Sansovino and the winning model was cast in bronze.

RELATED LITERATURE

F. Haskell and N. Penny, *Taste and the Antique*, New Haven and London 1981, pp. 243–47

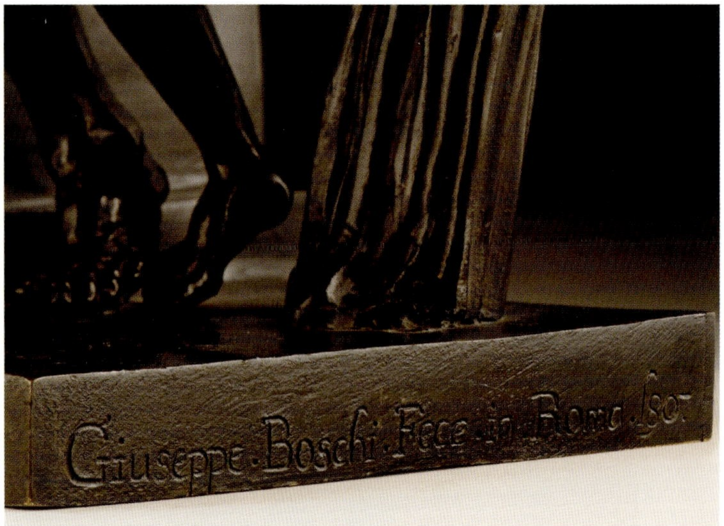

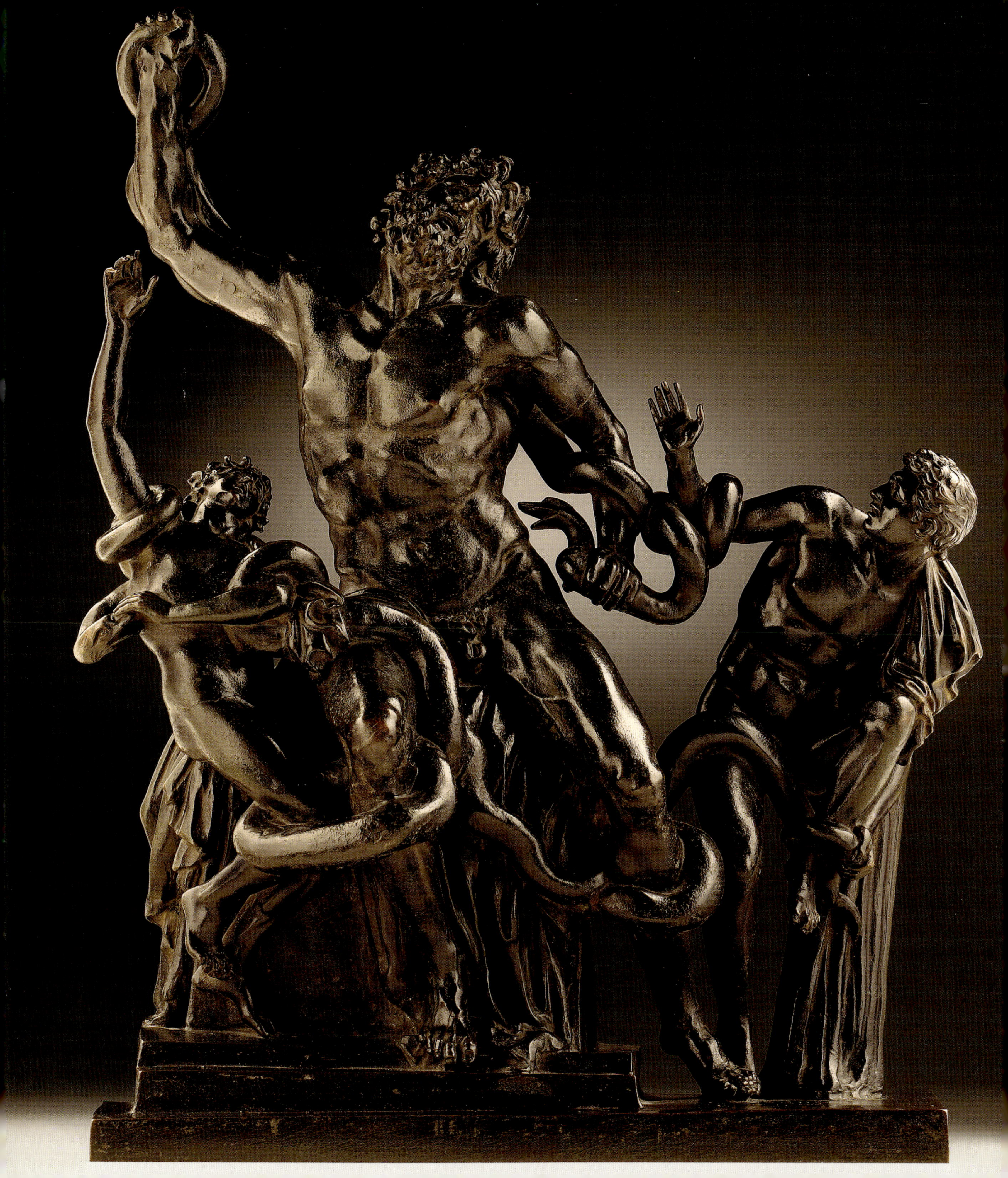

33. ADAMO TADOLINI (1788–1868)

Aeneas, Anchises and Ascanius

Terracotta

10 7⁄8 in. (27.8 cm) high

PROVENANCE: Reputedly by descent from the sculptor's own collection; collection of Dr Charles Avery

Adamo Tadolini was Bolognese by birth, but soon moved to Rome and became a favourite in the studio of Antonio Canova, who admired his understanding of classical proportions. Tadolini is generally considered to be Canova's most gifted pupil and heir to his legacy. In 1808 Tadolini won a prize for a terracotta relief representing *Venus giving Arms to Aeneas*, suggesting he was well informed on ancient mythological subjects. Canova was clearly very close to Tadolini, as he stood as guarantor for his studio in Rome.

The attribution of the present terracotta to Tadolini is based on stylistic grounds: it is directly influenced by Canova's classicism and by paintings of his time, most notably by Jacques-Louis David and alumni of the French Academy in Rome.

RELATED LITERATURE

T.F. Hufschmidt, *Tadolini: Adamo, Scipione, Giulio, Enrico: Quattro generazioni di scultori a Roma nei secoli XIX e XX*, Rome 1996

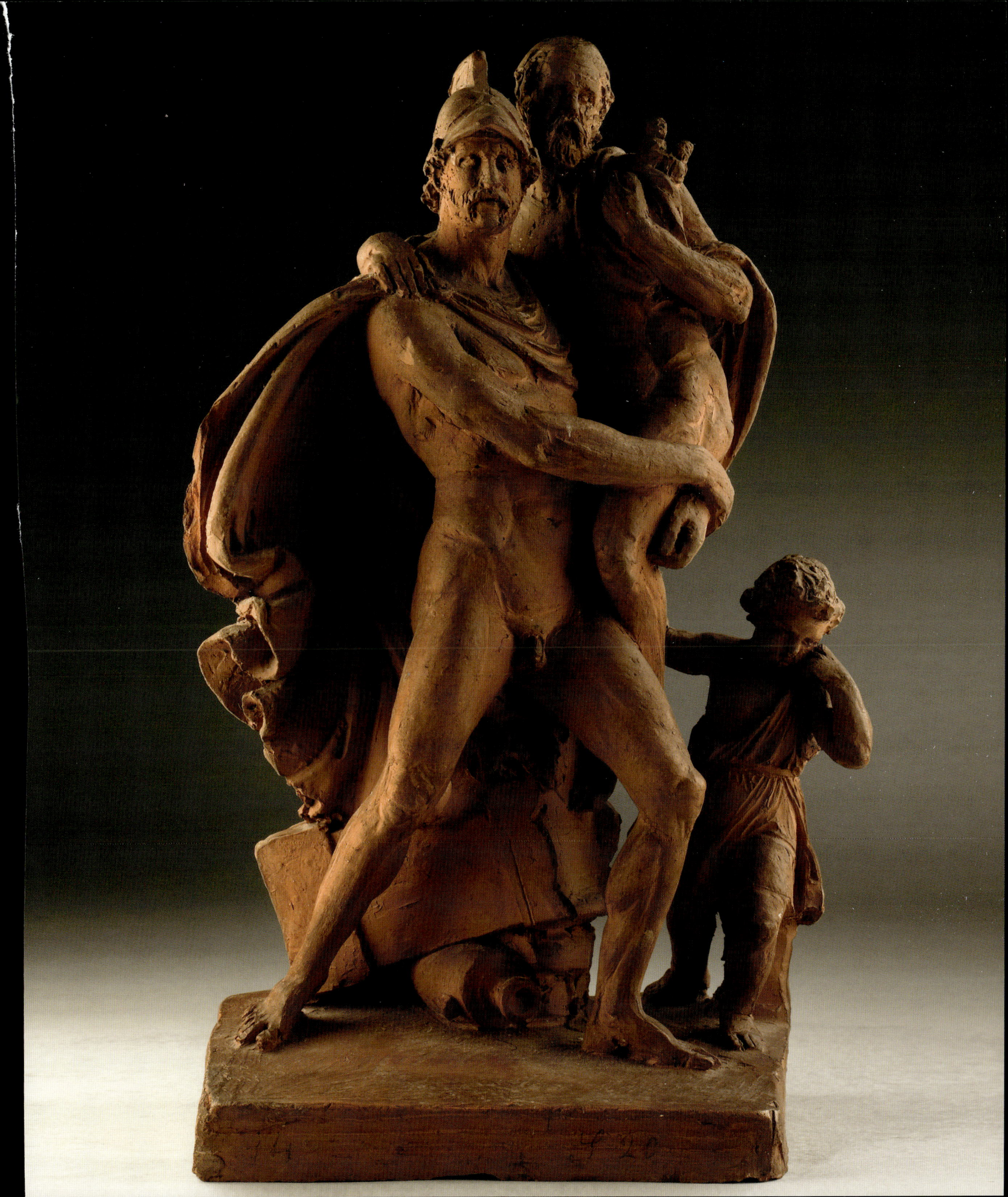

ISBN 978 1 903470 99 2

British Library Cataloguing in Publication Data
A catalogue record of this book is available from the British Library

Produced by Paul Holberton publishing
89 Borough High Street, London, SE1 1NL
www.paul-holberton.net

Designed by Peter Campbell
Photography by Doug Currie
Lithography and printing by e-graphic, Verona, Italy

FRONT COVER: Giambologna, *Prometheus bringing Fire to Mankind*, no. 9
BACK COVER: Jan Claudius de Cock, *A Pair of Figures representing Air and Fire*, no. 24
INSIDE FRONT FLAP: Pierre Petitot, *The Giustiniani Minerva*, no. 31
INSIDE BACK FLAP: François Girardon (workshop of), *Marsyas*, no. 19
FRONTISPIECE: Jean Raon (circle of), *A Bust of a Young Faun* (detail), no. 20